T3-BRL-626

WITHDRAWN

No longer the property of the
Boston Public Library.
Sale of this material benefits the Library

ROYAL EMPIRE SOCIETY IMPERIAL STUDIES.
General Editor:
ARTHUR PERCIVAL NEWTON, M.A., D.Lit., B.Sc., F.S.A.

No. 1.
Political Unrest in Upper Canada, 1815-1836.
By A. DUNHAM, PH.D.   9s. net.

No. 2.
The British West African Settlements, 1750-1821.
A Study in Local Administration.
By E. C. MARTIN, PH.D. With 2 maps.   7s. 6d. net.

No. 3.
**British Colonial Policy and the South African
Republics.** By C. W. DE KIEWEIT, M.A., PH.D
                                                       12s. 6d. net.
No. 4.
British Policy and Canada, 1774-1791.
A Study in Eighteenth-Century Trade Policy.
By GERALD S. GRAHAM, M.A., PH.D. With 2 maps.
                                                       10s. 6d. net.
No. 5.
Colonial Admiralty Jurisdiction in the 17th Century
By HELEN J. CRUMP, M.A., PH.D.   9s. net.

No. 6.
Education for Empire Settlement. A Study of Ju-
venile Migration. By ALEX. G. SCHOLES, B.A. (Melb.),
DIP. ED. (Melb.), PH.D. (Edin.)   7s. 6d. net.

No. 7.
The Provincial System in New Zealand, 1852-76.
By W. P. MORRELL, M.A., D.PHIL. With folding map.
                                                       10s. 6d. net.
No. 8.
**Railway and Customs Policies in South Africa,
1885-1910.** By JEAN VAN DER POEL, M.A., PH.D.
With folding map   7s. 6d. net.
No. 9.
The 1820 Settlers in South Africa. A Study in Brit-
ish Colonial Policy. By ISOBEL EIRLYS EDWARDS, M.A.
With two folding maps and two illustrations. 7s. 6d. net.
No. 10.
**Governor Arthur's Convict System, Van Diemen's
Land, 1824-36.** A Study in Colonization. By WILLIAM
DOUGLASS FORSYTH, B.A. With portrait.   7s. 6d. net.
No. 11.
Canada and the British Army 1846-1871. A Study in
the Practice of Responsible Government. By C. P.
STACEY, B.A., A.M., PH.D.   10s. 6d. net.
No. 12.
The Earth Goddess. A Study of Native Farming on the
West African Coast. By G. HOWARD JONES, M.A.
                                                       12s. 6d. net.
No. 13.
The Colonial Office. A History.
By HENRY L. HALL, M.A., PH.D. With four illustrations.
                                                       12s. 6d. net:
No. 14.
European Beginnings in West Africa, 1454-1578.
By JOHN W. BLAKE. With three maps.   10s. 6d. net.

IMPERIAL STUDIES, No. 15

General Editor :—A. P. NEWTON, M.A., D. Lit., B.Sc., F.S.A.,
Rhodes Professor of Imperial History in the University of London.

THE CRUCIAL PROBLEM OF
IMPERIAL DEVELOPMENT

[Conference on imperial development, London, 1937]

THE CRUCIAL PROBLEM

OF

IMPERIAL DEVELOPMENT

WITH A FOREWORD BY

THE RIGHT HON. MALCOLM MACDONALD, M.P.

H.M. Secretary of State for the Dominions

PUBLIC LIBRARY
OF THE
CITY OF BOSTON

PUBLISHED FOR THE ROYAL EMPIRE SOCIETY BY

LONGMANS, GREEN AND CO.

LONDON ★ NEW YORK ★ TORONTO

LONGMANS, GREEN AND CO. LTD.
39 PATERNOSTER ROW, LONDON, E.C.4
17 CHITTARANJAN AVENUE, CALCUTTA
53 NICOL ROAD, BOMBAY
36A MOUNT ROAD, MADRAS

LONGMANS, GREEN AND CO.
114 FIFTH AVENUE, NEW YORK
221 EAST 20TH STREET, CHICAGO
88 TREMONT STREET, BOSTON

LONGMANS, GREEN AND CO.
215 VICTORIA STREET, TORONTO

H C 246
. C 75
Copy 2

First Published 1938

Josiah H. Benton Fund
Aug. 31 1939
PUBLIC LIBRARY
OF THE
CITY OF BOSTON
2576. 82. 75
Sup.

Printed in Great Britain

FOREWORD

I am glad to have the opportunity of writing a foreword to the Record of the Conference on Imperial Development convened by the Royal Empire Society. It was a great disappointment to me that I was unavoidably prevented from taking the Chair at the opening meeting.

The Conference was planned on a scale embracing all parts of the British Empire and its general theme was developed by experts in a series of authoritative reviews. I am glad to see that the various aspects dealt with were considered from a wide standpoint, and in relation not merely to Imperial development, but also to the course of world trade. I am sure that this breadth of approach, if I may so describe it, was wise and right.

It is, I think, both significant and hopeful that the first Conference of this kind convened by the Royal Empire Society in its new hall should have been upon a subject of so general and important a character. I have no doubt that the published summary of the discussions will be of value to all who are engaged in the study of the economic and political problems facing the British Empire to-day.

MALCOLM MACDONALD.[1]

[1] MACDONALD, Rt. Hon. MALCOLM, P.C., M.P., son of the late Rt. Hon. J. Ramsay Macdonald, M.P. M.P. (Labour) for the Bassetlaw Division of Notts, 1929–31, (Nat. Lab.) for the same Division, 1931–35, and (Nat. Lab.) for Ross and Cromarty Division since Feb. 1936; Parliamentary Under-Sec. of State for the Dominions, 1931–5 ; Sec. of State for the Colonies, 1935–7 ; Sec. of State for the Dominions, 1937.

MESSAGE FROM THE HIGH COMMISSIONER FOR AUSTRALIA

(RT. HON. STANLEY M. BRUCE, C.H., M.C.)[1]

Our gratitude is due to the Royal Empire Society for its initiative in calling together the Conference on Empire Development at which the papers reprinted in this volume were read, and not least for arranging the programme so that special attention was called to the importance of higher levels of consumption.

Despite the fact that a Conference on the economic development of countries so different in their types of production and stages of progress as comprise the British Empire must necessarily have covered a diversity of problems, certain new and important currents of thought appear to underlie the speeches. The greatest achievement of the Conference was to have brought these ideas to the forefront.

The Empire's and the World's economic difficulties in the past few years have not been caused by problems of production. On the contrary, men, machinery and materials have been utilized at much less than their possible levels of output. The urgent problem of to-day is to ensure that consumers attain ever-rising standards of living, so that we avail ourselves to the full of our modern powers to produce.

To-day, both in the Empire and in many foreign countries, men's minds are turning towards what has been described as consumer economics. As one speaker said : " Economics is really the study of the relationship between consumption and production, and it is only worth studying when this is borne in mind ". We are beginning to realise that science has made

[1] BRUCE, Rt. Hon. Stanley Melbourne, C.H., M.C. High Commissioner for Australia since 1933. Commonwealth Treasurer, 1921–23. Prime Minister of Australia and Minister for External Affairs, 1923–29. Minister without Portfolio, 1932–33. Represented Australia at the Ottawa Conference and many International Conferences.

it possible for us to envisage the progressive conquest of poverty. This growing realisation is largely due to the nutrition campaign, and it is impossible to read the records of this Conference without realising the profound influence that Sir John Orr has exercised upon his day and generation.

Determined efforts to secure higher standards of living will provide an impetus to economic development and progress, and the Conference pointed out the importance of this aspect for Empire development. This thought was most admirably brought out by Mr. McDougall in the opening address, and it was further stressed by other speakers. The paper on India, for example, shows the importance of increased consumption if the economic problems of that vast and densely populated country are to be solved.

Although I was prevented at the last moment from attending this Conference, I have read these addresses with the utmost interest, and warmly commend them to public attention. I am convinced that the British Empire can make a great contri· bution towards the achievement of the inspiring objectives of securing much higher levels of health, happiness and efficiency through greater consumption. As Empire development must, to a considerable degree, run parallel with world development, the implementation of the policies which this Conference has been considering would give an example to the world of the methods by which prosperity and peace itself are to be attained.

S. M. BRUCE.

INTRODUCTION

THROUGHOUT the seventy years of its existence the Royal Empire Society (or, as it used to be called, the Royal Colonial Institute) has emphasised above all the essential unity of the Empire-Commonwealth and its problems. It has provided a forum wherein men from every part of the King's Realms could discuss the solution of those problems and bring to bear upon them vast and varied experience gained in many capacities. Statesmen, Governors, Civil Servants, Politicians of every shade of opinion, representatives of commerce, manufacturers, agriculturists, Trade Union leaders and men of every profession have contributed their knowledge and ideas to the common stock, and thus upon occasion the Society has been enabled to aid in the formation of public opinion upon our imperial problems with an influence that was widely based. The re-housing of the Society in its fine new building, to whose erection and adornment almost every Government throughout the Empire has contributed, affords the opportunity of continuing and extending this vital side of its work on a larger scale, and in November, 1937, the Chairman and Council invited many persons of acknowledged position and influence to meet in Conference to discuss the crucial problem that faces the nations of the Empire to-day.

The British Empire—the United Kingdom, the Dominions, India and the Colonies, Protectorates and Mandates—constitutes the greatest group of countries in the world. It comprises twenty-six per cent of the land surface of the world, contains twenty-two per cent of the world's population and conducts thirty-one per cent of the world's trade.

The most vital interest of the whole Empire is peace, and a strong British Empire is, therefore, one of the greatest factors for world peace.

The Conference was concerned not with the military power of the Empire nor with its foreign relations, but with its economic strength and development. Without economic strength it cannot exert the powerful influence for peace and progress that the world needs to-day.

The Empire has never been, and cannot become, a closed economic system, for it needs world markets and requires world trade. Hence increased prosperity within the Empire will benefit not only Empire countries but all nations. The Empire can, therefore, make a great contribution to the economic appeasement of the world.

Along what lines must we act if we are to secure a great increase in Empire prosperity? The obvious answer is that we must increase consumption, and the crucial problem is to find how this can be achieved. The scope for increased demand for food, clothing, houses and for every sort of manufactured goods is immense. There is within the Empire no lack of resources—in men, capital or Nature's gifts—to fill those needs. But increased consumption is dependent upon increased purchasing power, which again is dependent upon enlarging the real national income of every portion of the Empire. This must be achieved through increased efficiency of production in the broadest sense, including the fuller use of existing capital and labour force, technical reform and the improvement of distribution and exchange mechanism.

The purpose of the Conference was to consider the relation of consumption and production, practicable methods for stimulating both, and the effects which the successful attainment of these objectives would have upon the prosperity of Empire countries and upon world trade.

The discussions of the Conference were confined to those who had been invited to attend and its proceedings were not reported in the public Press, but the Council were of the opinion that the papers presented and the comments they elicited were of such value as contributions to thought upon the problem dealt with that they demand wide circulation not only throughout the countries of the Empire but generally. The proceedings of the Conference have therefore been collected and are here presented to form a basis for wider discussion in the hope that they will stimulate and inspire others to direct their thoughts from new angles to the problem that is of such vital interest both to the British Empire and the world.

For nearly twenty years we seem to have been wandering round and round in a vicious circle of ideas derived from conditions that have passed. The contributors to the Conference have sought to break out from the circle and attack the problem in a different way. They were all persons of authority in their own spheres, and it has seemed fitting to indicate in footnotes attached to their contributions the experience which entitled them to speak. To the proceedings of the main Conference there is added a summary account of certain discussions on the same subject that took place at a subsequent smaller Conference of younger men and women from many parts of the Empire. This junior Conference was organised under the ægis of the Council of the Royal Empire Society by a Committee of students working in British universities who were anxious to discuss together the imperial problems which inevitably will fall to men and women of their age to tackle when they in their turn come to positions of influence. Conditions of space have prevented a full report of the proceedings of the Junior Conference, but it has seemed to be of interest to include a summary indicating the line its discussions took and this has therefore been presented as an annex to the main report.

It may be added that the reports of their contributions have been submitted to each member of the Conference who took part in the discussions and have been approved by them before publication. For the collected report as a whole, the Royal Empire Society alone is responsible. No resolutions were submitted and none were reached, for to formulate conclusions lay beyond the purpose of the Conference. That was only to secure the ventilation of ideas, and it is to place those ideas before a wider public that the proceedings are now published.

CONTENTS

I

THE PROBLEM STATED. THE DOMINIONS AND THE UNITED KINGDOM

Tuesday, November 23rd, 1937. Morning Session

THE Secretary of State for the Dominions had promised to preside, but he was called to attend the Conference of the Powers in Brussels as British delegate, and in his absence the Chair was taken by the Chairman of the Royal Empire Society who opened the proceedings of the Conference with a speech of welcome.

Sir ARCHIBALD WEIGALL[1]: On behalf of the Council of the Royal Empire Society, I offer you a warm welcome to this Conference in the only building in the British Empire in whose erection and adornment all the Overseas Dominions, India and the Colonies, with the exception of the Irish Free State, have had a hand.

The object of the Conference is to direct your minds to the stimulation of world consumption in general and economic appeasement in particular. I do not want to elaborate it at all beyond saying this, that at this particular moment I think everybody who sits back and thinks at all, when they realise the fluidity of affairs in Europe, the periodic high explosive reports of dictators, and the change produced in inter-imperial relations by the passage of the Statute of Westminster, will agree that all these do collectively make it more and more imperative that we should have the closest possible co-operation within the British Empire. It seems to me, as a humble outsider, that to promote that co-operation to-day has become

---

[1] WEIGALL, Sir Archibald, K.C.M.G., Chairman of the Royal Empire Society, Served in South Africa, 1902. M.P. (Unionist) Horncastle Division of Lincs.. 1911–20. Chairman of Food Survey Board, Ministry of Food, 1917–20. Member of Select Committee on National Expenditure. President, Agricultural Organisation Society, 1919. Governor of South Australia, 1920–22. President Land Agents' Society, 1934. Member of the Council of the Royal Agricultural Society.

B

something that is every man's job in this country, because it
seems to be the only sort of solid foundation on which one can
hope to establish an economic, ordered life in an atmosphere
of international peace.

What has alarmed and amazed me recently is both to read
and hear speeches from presumably fairly well-informed people,
all totally oblivious of the fact that the Statute of Westminster
is now on the Statute Book. They seem to credit the British
Government with powers that it does not possess and they
accuse the Secretary of State for the Dominions of inertia when
in reality independent action by him, even if it were possible,
which it is not, would be fraught with the greatest danger. I
do feel that it is essential that we should bring it home to our
fellow-countrymen what is the relationship between the Self-
Governing Dominions and our own Government here, and
secondly—and equally important—the relationship between
the Self-Governing Dominions themselves.

I have an apology to make. The Secretary of State for the
Dominions was looking forward with great interest, I know, to
taking the Chair for us, but Mr. MacDonald has been sent for
by the Nine Power Conference in Brussels, and you have to
put up with me in his place. Let me say here how enormously
grateful I am to the Secretary of State and all the Officials in
the Dominions Office for the unfailing help they have given
us in arranging this Conference. The Colonial Office and the
offices of the High Commissioners for the Dominions and India
have aided us without stint and we desire to acknowledge their
help most warmly.

Before calling upon the principal speaker at this session, I
would like to read a message that we have received from Sir
Josiah Stamp, who had hoped to take part in our proceedings,
but has been unavoidably prevented by official business. He
says :

(Sir JOSIAH STAMP : " I am very glad to see that a comprehensive review of the problems of Imperial Development is
being undertaken at this particular moment. We have before
us the accepted fact that we cannot begin on the next important stage of world prosperity without greater freedom
of international trade—so much is practically common
ground. But what is not so readily recognised is that we

cannot expect to get any *material* improvement of inter-empire trade except by a process which moves *in harmony* with world trade interests and not across them. If this is so, those who are interested in Empire development must be at least equally interested in world development.

The key to world development at the moment is example and leadership. Towards this, Anglo-American co-operation and the recently announced negotiations for a trade agreement are easily the most important factors. Therefore, it follows that a favourable development of Anglo-American trade is a definite step towards the success of the movement for larger Empire trade. But here is the heart of the paradox. The chief difficulty in negotiating the Anglo-American Treaty is that of keeping the integrity of Imperial preference. Anglo-American agreements are thus both the greatest help and the greatest difficulty in Empire development. Neither of these ideals must be given up, but the practical course must satisfy them both. It is useless to consider small gains in Empire development which jeopardise world development, because failure here must in turn react. If the Conference can throw any light on methods of stimulating inter-Empire trade which are not at the same time inimical to Anglo-American development and the removal of trade barriers generally, they will render an immense service. But of one thing I am quite certain, that is, to focus entirely upon Empire questions without reference to the larger environment in which they are to be developed, is to achieve a limited success which will ultimately defeat our main object. In developing the Empire through special trade relations, I do not think we are now running counter to what the world expects, because the world has just come to appreciate more than ever before the value of the stability of the Empire as a force making for peace and prosperity, and they will, therefore, be willing to accept any application of the principle of Imperial Preference that has fairly and squarely taken account of world issues and freer trade."

Now that we are able to meet in this wonderful building through the generosity of the Empire, I do feel it ought to become the focal point for study and discussion of all Imperial affairs. This is the first big Conference here, and I hope we shall have at least yearly ones coming on from now onwards, in order that the platform of the Royal Empire Society can be a forum for discussion, and the fount from which we can create a really informed opinion upon imperial matters amongst our fellow-countrymen here and overseas.

It is my duty to introduce Mr. McDougall, whom you all know. His unceasing efforts at Geneva as a member of the Consultative Economic Committee of the League of Nations enable me to call him " the champion of economic appeasement ", for there has been no one who has done more towards the achievement of economic appeasement than Mr. McDougall

Mr. F. L. McDOUGALL[1]: It is much too soon for anyone to claim any credit for the development of the ideas expressed in the phrase " Economic Appeasement". It is, however, through conferences of this sort that such ideas will become current. I take it that this is the first conference ever held to discuss Empire development from the standpoint of consumption and production, but there is no doubt that the time is ripe for the fullest exploration of this avenue of approach.

As the general note accompanying the invitation to the Conference pointed out, the British Empire comprises twenty-six per cent of the land surfaces of the world, contains twenty-two per cent of the world's population, and conducts thirty-one per cent of the world's trade. Its territories are scattered throughout every continent and its coasts are washed by every ocean.

This is not the occasion when we should discuss the vulnerability of the Empire nor its methods of defence save in so far as we should recognise the dependence of our united military resources upon our economic strength.

We can, however, start with one axiom which will not, I think, be challenged, namely, that it is only through our

[1] McDOUGALL, F. L., C.M.G., F.S.S. Australian Representative on and (since 1935) Chairman of the Imperial Economic Committee. Lived in South Africa and has been engaged in fruit-farming in Australia. One of the Economic advisers to the Australian Prime Ministers at the Imperial Economic Conferences, 1923, 1932, and the Imperial Conferences, 1926, 1930. Member of the Empire Marketing Board. Member of the Consultative Economic Committee of the League of Nations and of the Permanent Committee of the International Institute of Agriculture.

continued growth and development that we shall be able to maintain both the Commonwealth and the Empire.

At first sight, it may not seem at all easy to maintain progressive development at a time when the leading authorities on population trends are assuring us that the growth of population in the United Kingdom and in the Dominions is slowing down and may be expected to become stationary within a relatively short period. There is no doubt that this will be the case, given the maintenance of present social trends. I am, however, by no means convinced that if we could bring about a general improvement in social standards and less handicaps for parents, women will continue to regard motor-cars or wireless sets as more amusing and desirable than babies.

Nevertheless, this Conference must face the present fact of declining apparent fertility. Statements have not infrequently been made by eminent economists that the declining rate of population growth will bring us face to face with surplus capacity not only in industry but in agriculture. We have, of course, been familiar with surplus capacity in industry during depressions. We have even seen a World Monetary and Economic Conference almost unanimous about the need for restriction of certain forms of agricultural production. These things being so, it is indeed high time for us to study consumption and see whether present trends are really likely to increase the difficulties of Empire development.

In studying consumption we shall have to consider many things in addition to food, but we may well commence with food, first because of its intrinsic importance both to the consumer and the producer and, secondly, because through the development of the nutrition movement, we now have a wealth of information at our disposal.

The *Listener*, the journal of the British Broadcasting Corporation, recently published a talk by Mr. Loveday, the Director of the Financial and Economic Intelligence Sections of the League of Nations. Mr. Loveday's section had been responsible for the preparation of the Final Report of the League Nutrition Committee and he had been asked to broadcast about this report. In this talk Mr. Loveday said :

" This nutrition campaign seems to me to be of paramount

importance not only on account of its immediate object, which is to improve the standard of living, but also on account of the influence it is likely to have on our whole economic outlook. Ever since the time of Adam Smith economic thought has centred round the art of production or the conditions of citizens as producers. The nutrition movement reflects the first serious endeavour, certainly on an international scale, to consider the economics not of production but of consumption.

The second point that I want to mention is somewhat similar. Economists have concentrated in the past on problems of production. Production of what ? Production of an endless series of inanimate objects. Those concerned with this nutrition campaign say : ' No, what you should really try to produce first is the best possible human beings— the best possible citizens '.''

Mr. Loveday's words may perhaps supply a key to the problem of Empire development.

What is the relationship between the consumption of food and the quantity and quality of human life in the United Kingdom. During the centuries preceding the industrial revolution, the population of these islands remained almost stagnant ; indeed from the fifteenth to the middle of the eighteenth century the total increase was only about 1,000,000. Compare this position with what happened in the nineteenth century. Between 1801 and 1901 the population of England and Wales increased by 23.6 millions in spite of a nett loss by emigration of about 9,000,000 persons.

What was the cause of the extraordinary change ? It cannot be ascribed to an increase in births per head of the marriageable women but to dramatic falls in the infantile and adult mortality rates.

The Expert Committee of the League of Nations ascribes these changes to two types of causes, one of which it describes as ' negative ' and the other as ' positive ' factors.

The ' negative ' factors were those which led to a greater control of disease, sanitation, pure water supplies, immunisation and the segregation of infectious cases such as, vaccination for smallpox.

The main positive factor was the increasing abundance of food supplies due to the opening up of the new lands in the Americas and in Australia and New Zealand.

In point of historical time, the upward surge of population commenced with the increase in food supplies purchased with the manufactures of the new mechanised industries and the great discoveries in medical science which came rather later in the century.

Hence Burke had the fullest warrant for that eloquent passage in his speech on conciliation with America when he declared in the House of Commons on March 22nd, 1775 :

" For some time past, the old world has been fed from the new. The scarcity which you have felt would have been a desolating famine, if this child of your old age [America] with a true filial piety, with a Roman charity, had not put the full breast of its youthful exuberance to the mouth of its exhausted parent."

As the Nutrition Report states, the population increase and the decline in the death rate from a number of diseases, especially tuberculosis, had started and got well under way before the new medical and bacteriological discoveries had been made or applied.

During the nineteenth century, the sanitary reforms initiated by Chadwick in the 40's, and later the researches of Pasteur and a host of other workers gave us ever better control over disease.

These two sets of factors, the ' positive,' that is to say more abundant and varied food and better social conditions, and the ' negative ', disease control, resulted in a marked prolongation of the life of the individual. The average Englishman born in the 1840's could only expect to attain 40 years of age, whereas in 1920–22 his expectation of life had increased to 54–56 years, and has since increased still more.

It is rather satisfactory from an Empire point of view to be able to record what I am going to say now. To-day, if the infantile and adult death rates of countries are compared, it will be found that two parts of the British Commonwealth—New Zealand and Australia—have lower rates than any country in the world. It is impossible not to connect this fact directly with the relatively high average standard of living in both of these Dominions where smaller differences between individual incomes exist than in most countries.

Professor J. B. S. Haldane, has, in a recent essay, thrown into high relief this great achievement of the British peoples of the Antipodes. He writes :

" I am a citizen of the British Empire, which includes the great Dominions. My highbrow friends complain that the Dominions have produced little great art or literature. I answer that at least they have done something unique. Before the war the average expectation of life of a baby born in New Zealand was sixty years, in Australia fifty-seven years, in Denmark, the next healthiest country, fifty-six years. England also ran. Since then other countries have caught up to a large extent, but New Zealand and Australia still seem to be leading. I am proud to belong to a Commonwealth which has won the first and second places in the great race against death."

That these increases in the quantity of human life have not been made at the expense of general virility and physique, i.e., its quality, is clearly shown by the increase in the height and weight of the average citizen and by the steady lowering of all records of athletic achievements.

Neither can it be maintained that the moral fibre has been detrimentally affected. Under the grim test of war, it was found that our divisions were capable of sustaining the heaviest losses and yet of retaining their fighting qualities. I vividly recall an Australian Division losing 8,000 men, eighty per cent of its effectives, in one tour of the line but after short rest and reinforcement, being still capable of vigorous offensive action. That particular example is by no means unique, but if you examine the history of war, you will find that there are very few examples where large masses of troops suffered the losses which they suffered during the last war, and were still able to continue to fight.

So much for the progress made during the last 150 years, progress partly due to medical science but at least as largely due to increased consumption.

What of the future ? It would, I think, be generally agreed that it would be optimistic to anticipate that the progress of medical science during the next fifty years will be able to accomplish the same striking effects upon the incidence of disease as in the past. So much has already been accomplished in combating such great destroyers of life as cholera, plague, smallpox and enteric, that future progress can hardly be expected to show such spectacular returns.

This means that we can probably expect less from the ' negative ' factors than in the past but is this equally true where the ' positive ' factors are concerned ?

To answer this question it is necessary to turn from the consideration of the vital statistics of nations as a whole to comparisons between the mortality rates of different districts within the same country. A study of this sort immediately reveals the immense scope that exists for future progress on the ' positive ' side.

The Registrar-General's returns for the United Kingdom show what is called the ' local adjusted death rate ' in comparison to the national death rate. These adjusted death rates mean rates that have been adjusted to eliminate the factor of the differing age composition in the various localities.

On this basis, when the death rate for England and Wales is taken as 1, we find that if you take areas of very considerable general prosperity, such as Ealing, Cambridge, St. Albans and Chislehurst, the death rate is from .7 to .8, and in one case, Welwyn Garden City, falls as low as .53. On the other hand, in the poverty stricken areas such as Durham, Glamorgan and parts of Lancashire, the figure rises to 1.25 and even to as high as 1.4.

If infantile mortality figures are taken, a similar picture is obtained. With the infantile death rate for the whole country returned as 59 per 1,000, the prosperous districts, such as those that I have mentioned, return rates of from 32 up to 45 per 1,000, while the poverty stricken areas have rates varying from 70 up to as high as 109.

These figures indicate that, as has already been pointed out in the Nutrition Report of the League of Nations, " the general mortality rates in poor districts are fifty per cent higher than in the wealthier ones, while tuberculosis mortality is almost four times as high in the former as in the latter, and the corresponding proportion of infantile mortality is as 2 to 1."

A study of these figures forces us to the conclusion that poverty is linked with malnutrition, disease and premature death.

It would, of course, be impossible to maintain that the only cause of the difference between the vital statistics of well-to-do and poverty stricken areas is the one factor of differences in consumption. Many other factors enter into the picture.

Nevertheless, since to-day in all parts of the country there are very nearly equal conditions in regard to purity of water supply, general district sanitation and the segregation of infectious diseases, the two factors remaining which could account for such marked differences as those cited are nutrition and housing ; in other words two aspects of the general problem of consumption.

I have not been able to obtain comparable statistics of regional districts in the Dominions, and it is improbable that such marked contrasts would be found in countries where the national income is spread more evenly over all classes. There are, however, very marked contrasts between mortality rates in Montreal and Toronto, and the same general trend that is so apparent in England and Wales would undoubtedly be found, although in a lesser degree, throughout the Dominions and indeed in all countries in the world.

These facts indicate the immense scope for further improvement that exists as we discover means for bringing about increased consumption of food, of clothing, and of building materials, and thus ensuring to the whole of our peoples the conditions which science has placed so easily within our physical grasp.

It is for other speakers to deal with the problem of consumption in parts of the Empire other than the United Kingdom and the Dominions. It may, however, be appropriate for me to say a very few words about the position of consumption in the world outside the British Empire.

In certain countries, such as Scandinavia and Holland, you find conditions which approximate closely to those existing in Australia and in New Zealand, and there you find that the high relative general prosperity is closely reflected in good vital statistics.

The position in Germany and the United States is somewhat

inferior to that of England and Wales, but on the same general level as Scotland. France and Italy occupy a definitely lower level, but below them we find the whole group of countries of Central and Eastern Europe where the condition of nutrition and general consumption of all commodities among both the urban proletarist and the agricultural peasants represents a level of poverty which is only parallelled among the coloured population of the Southern States of America and only exceeded in the Far East.

In such countries adult death rates are high and infantile mortality reaches figures which run up to 200 and even higher per 1,000 live births.

The poverty in the Far East, and particularly in China, is well known, and I need only cite here the reply of the Chinese Government to the official questionnaire sent by the League Committee on Nutrition which started with the words " Generally speaking most Chinese are suffering from malnutrition all the time."

The League Committee on Nutrition received a large number of replies to its questionnaire. In most cases, the Governments were at pains to show that malnutrition was not serious in their country, but the Chinese reply was extremely frank.

I am mentioning these facts about foreign countries because at the conclusion of this address I shall have some remarks to make about the importance of the British Commonwealth using its combined political and economic influence in co-operation with other great nations, such as the United States, in order to bring about general improvements in standards of living throughout the world.

It is essential, in my view, that we should recollect that, as the general note of the invitation to this Conference indicated, " the Empire has never been and cannot become a closed economic system, for it needs world markets and requires world trade."

Having dealt at some considerable length with the problems of consumption, we must now return to glance at the problem of production.

I should like to emphasise that production does not just mean the growing of crops or the conversion of raw materials into manufactured articles. It means the whole system of production and distribution from the raw material, say, grass and oilcake in the case of milk, down to the delivery of the milk at the consumer's door, or the production of a suit of clothes from the wool on the back of an Australian merino sheep until the tailor has delivered a new suit carefully packed to our houses or flats.

This problem of production and its relationship to consumption will be dealt with more fully than I can hope to do by Professor Noel Hall in a later session.

At this stage in the Conference, however, I desire to draw attention to the immense scope that still exists for increasing the efficiency and hence in reducing the real costs both of production and of distribution. During the past 150 years enormous progress has been made. Progress is due in the main to the application of the results of scientific research in physics, chemistry and biology.

The first stage was the opening up of the new virgin lands in the overseas countries through the development of the railway, the steamship and later the internal combustion engine. Progress in these directions was particularly rapid during the middle fifty years of the nineteenth century; indeed towards the end of the century a position was reached in which it appeared improbable, on the basis of the then existing knowledge, that further extensive progress would be found possible.

This led, as most of us know, to that remarkable forecast of Sir William Crookes, who pointed out at a British Association meeting in the 1890's that unless great progress was made in the fixation of atmospheric nitrogen to supply fertilisers, the world would be faced with a wheat shortage in the 1930's.

Well, the fixation of atmospheric nitrogen has been accomplished, though very little has been applied to the wheat lands of the world, and yet, in 1931, Crookes' critical year, I found myself sitting at an International Conference in Rome to consider how to regulate the production of wheat which was becoming superabundant for the existing effective world demand. I would place great emphasis on the word ' *effective* '.

I mention this example because it is typical of the food position generally. At the very time when Crookes spoke, patient work, of which he had no knowledge, was being carried out by plant breeders in Canada and in Australia, to evolve early maturing wheats for the northern districts of Canada and drought resistant varieties for semi-arid areas. The success of the plant breeder added hundreds of thousands of square miles to the potential granaries of the world.

Similar, though less striking because so far less generally applied, progress has been made in the breeding of grasses and clovers and indeed of the great majority of the economic plants of the world.

The effects of improved transport has also been very great. In the 1840's McCulloch, the economist, declared that no meat, even in a salted form, had ever come from South America nor ever would. Yet, to-day, we are faced with the problem of supplies slightly more abundant than the *effective* existing demand can accommodate, not only from South America but from New Zealand and Australia.

In regard to manufactured requirements, there is no known physical limit to the extent to which our increasing demand cannot be met.

It is only necessary to consider the effects of mass production, whether it be on the prices of manufactured goods as varied as motor-cars or men's suits, to realise the progress that has already been made in increased efficiency.

So here, again, on the production side we have a somewhat similar picture to that which exists in regard to consumption, great progress and yet immense scope for further improvement. We even find, in regard to production, the problem of what I might call backward areas. I suggest that the backward areas on the side of production are mainly to be found in agriculture and in distribution.

In the case of agriculture, the progress in the adoption of technical improvements is much slower than in industry. This is due, in part, to the multiplicity of small units of agricultural production, i.e., the farms, and to the inevitable difficulties of adequate agricultural credit, partly because agriculture is to many farmers rather a way of life than an economic enterprise, partly to the inherent conversatism of the average farmer even in the newer countries.

The result is that whereas in manufacturing industries new inventions may be generally adopted within a few years of their discovery, in agriculture the time-lag before general application may be achieved is often one of several decades.

Add to this the factor of the varying personal capacity of the farmer and it is not surprising to find the widest discrepancies in the costs of production.

The Australian Royal Commission on Wheat found after a careful examination of costs on 524 farms that whereas sixty per cent of the sample produced at prime costs of between 2s. 2d. and 3s. 10d. per bushel (prime costs excluding interest charges) the lowest cost fringe produced at 1s. and 2s. per bushel, while at the other end of the scale the high cost fringe had costs ranging from 4s. up to 15s. per bushel.

Studies of milk production costs in England show variations from 6d. per gallon up to 15 pence. A recent study by Cambridge University into pig-keeping costs in East Anglia show that, while on the sample taken, the average cost of producing £100 worth of pigs was £82, the most profitable farms had an average cost of £69 and the least profitable £113.

Differences of prime costs of this order cannot exist in manufacturing industry, since here the less efficient firms would rapidly be eliminated, but in agriculture the marginal producer manages to carry on for years, and it often seems that Government policy is based not on the requirements of the more efficient farm units but on those whose efficiency is below the average.

There are also marked contrasts between the prices which are regarded as satisfactory by the agriculture of different parts of the Empire. This is a controversial point and I will touch on it lightly. Thus, the Australian grazier would be well content with from £9 to £10 for a young steer, while the English farmer needs twice that figure.

I will not give further examples of such differences, but will merely point out that this is an important factor which must be taken into account when considering Empire development from the standpoint of the standard of living.

I have suggested that in the distributive processes we shall find another type of backward area so far as efficiency is concerned. Here the causes may be a multiplicity of competing and overlapping agencies, or the tendency to increase in costs through spreading the charge of expensive methods of delivery and credit to all consumers. Everyone here will be familiar with evidence of such practices and I will not attempt to go into any details.

Before attempting to make any constructive suggestions on the problem before us, I had better briefly summarise the position which we have now reached.

My points are as follows :

(i) That the Empire can only be maintained if we find the means to secure its continuous growth and development, or, in other words, if we, as a Commonwealth, do our full part in increasing general world prosperity.

(ii) That, although we are faced by the problems of decreasing apparent fertility, there is enormous scope for increased consumption if we are to secure to all our peoples the standards of living within our physical grasp.

(iii) That one of the most important ways of achieving these objectives is through increased efficiency in production and distribution, and that the scope for this is particularly marked where food is concerned.

What then are the practical lines of Policy which seem to emerge from a study of this problem ?

It is agreed that the Empire must be further developed, but there is little faith that much can be accomplished through migration schemes.

Is it not possible for Empire Governments boldly to define their principal economic objectives as being the improvement of the standards of living of their peoples ?

Such a suggestion might be met by assurances that the welfare of the whole people of each Empire nation is already the objective of all economic thought and of each Empire Government.

In a vague way this may conceivably be the case, although any study of Parliamentary debates in any Empire country, of Government declarations, or indeed of the pronouncements of the leaders of economic thought would tend to indicate that the interests of special groups of producers, perhaps not unnaturally, take precedence over the interests of the whole nation.

In other words, that we are all still wedded to ‘ producer ’ rather than to ‘ consumer ’ economics.

Public definition of the objective of our Governments to secure a progressive betterment of living standards might have marked effects on Empire development and might have international repercussions to which I shall again refer.

The necessary corollary of any such determination would be tne formulation of what may either be described as optimum standards in relation to food, housing, etc., or what might perhaps be as fittingly described as the decent minimum standard of a nation determined to secure the best available life for the whole of its people.

The Technical Commission on Nutrition of the League of Nations has already laid down for us such an optimum standard so far as food is concerned.

This standard, if achieved, would require for Great Britain, to take two examples only, an increase of liquid milk consumption which would not only absorb the whole of the present milk supply but would require a sixty per cent increase in the dairy herds of the United Kingdom, and a more than doubling of its egg production.

The effect of attempting to apply a decent minimum to the housing standards of any Empire country would have marked repercussions on the building material and the iron and steel trades.

Let us suppose that our Governmerts found it possible to accept national and Imperially concerted policies on the standard of living. What practical steps would it then be necessary for them to take ?

Having regard to the present distribution of the national income, they would certainly have to be prepared to go further along the path already indicated by such measures as milk for school children and for mothers, school meals, subsidised housing, etc.—in other words, it would mean an expansion of certain types of social services.

There must, however, be a limit to such measures and at a time when national resources in this country and in certain of the Dominions are being heavily drawn upon for rearmament, the limit might not be very elastic.

We must also realise that if we are to make any substantial further increase in social services or to secure a more equitable distribution of the national income through better wages, it will be necessary to secure international collaboration on as wide a scale as possible.

No single country can afford to go far ahead of its competitors without running some risk of loss of competitive power.

For this reason I attach a good deal of importance to the work of the League of Nations on Nutrition and to the League enquiry into Standards of Living that is about to commence.

A more vital and dynamic type of policy than direct action to increase consumption would be a determination to secure progressive increases in the efficiency of production and distribution.

In other words, that we should attempt to correlate our almost unlimited productive powers with the real potential demand.

Such a decision would imply the utilisation of the whole power of the State to promote efficiency, and there are many ways in which this can be done, especially in agriculture and distribution, to use those powers to protect and foster branches of industry and agriculture capable of adding real wealth to the community, and to withhold State assistance from such branches whose costs of production could not be reduced within a few years to levels at which the sale of their products would not impose any considerable burden upon the community as a whole.

This is a doctrine which would present political difficulties both in the United Kingdom and the Dominions, but one which, if jointly undertaken, would have great effects upon national wealth, technical efficiency and on the standards of living.

Considerations of national defence and perhaps of social interest might, in certain instances, impose some limitations on the application of this principle. The test of the validity of such limitations should, however, be real, and the touchstone should be that in every instance the national interest should take precedence of sectional interests.

There will be general agreement that there is no physical bar to the nations of the Commonwealth setting out to achieve these optimum standards for the peoples. What about the question of money ? When we come to the question of money, this is a very controversial subject, on which I am in no sense an authority.

Here I feel we come to a point at which we shall find that if we are to achieve the progress that can be accomplished, it will be essential to secure co-operation from countries outside the Empire and in particular from the United States of America.

c

I refuse to believe that progressive increases in the production and consumption of real wealth cannot be financed.

I think we can regard money as the lubricant of the economic machine, and that given proper directives from Governments, there is plenty of ability in the Treasuries and Central Banks to devise a sufficiently adequate lubrication system for the extension of our economic activities.

Isolated action in the monetary field, however, even by so great an entity as the British Commonwealth, might lead to difficulties, and for this reason the widest possible basis of collaboration should be sought.

Thus we reach from a purely Empire standpoint the need for international collaboration.

It would, of course, have been easy for me to have shown how far Empire industries, whether industrial in the United Kingdom or agricultural in the Dominions, require world markets. I could have cited Lancashire cotton, Yorkshire wool, Tyneside or Clydeside ship-building, Canadian wheat or newsprint, Australian wool and wheat, and in the near future New Zealand and Australian mutton and lamb, and butter.

I have deliberately avoided these issues, since they are all covered by my general thesis concerning the standard of living.

What then might be the effect on our international relations of policies along the lines we have been envisaging ?

The United Kingdom and the United States of America have just announced their intention of formally commencing negotiations for a commercial agreement. Everybody recognises that this is a momentous decision, and everyone also knows that in the forthcoming discussions the Dominions will be deeply concerned.

It is inevitable that the negotiations should be concerned with tariff concessions on certain articles in which special interests will fight to secure the reduction or retention of certain rates, that the preferential margins arranged at Ottawa will be subjected to challenge and to possible review.

The atmosphere thus engendered may not prove ideal for the development of those closer relations between the Commonwealth and the United States of America that are so urgently needed in the interest not only of World peace but also of world prosperity.

Would it not be possible to add to these necessary but rather small-scale discussions about rates of duty the larger considerations already envisaged by both Governments in their Tripartite Declaration on Monetary Policy of September, 1936.

In that declaration the Governments of the United Kingdom, the United States of America and France declared that " they would foster those conditions which will safeguard peace and will best contribute to the restoration of order in international economic relations, and to pursue a policy which will tend to promote prosperity in the world and to improve the standard of living."

Could there be a better corollary to the successful outcome of the negotiations now to be formally commenced than for the Governments of the United Kingdom and the United States of America to declare that, in collaboration with the Governments of the Dominions, they were determined actively to consult together and with any other Government which was prepared to co-operate, to devise means to secure for their respective peoples a rising standard of living, and their belief that this would increase the prosperity of the whole world.

To-day we must recognise that nothing goes unchallenged. Our democratic institutions are challenged, our economic system is challenged, the British Empire itself is not unchallenged. We cannot afford to neglect any means of defence, but surely our best defence is to prove that under systems of political and economic liberty we can achieve for our Empire peoples and for the peoples of any nations which will collaborate with us, conditions of life, opportunities for individual development and happiness which cannot be equalled by any other systems, whether Fascist or Communist.

The discussion was opened by :

LORD BLEDISLOE[1]: I desire, after listening to my old friend and colleague, Mr. McDougall, to emphasise the broadminded outlook which his extremely interesting and illuminating address has made clear. I think Mr. McDougall and I last met many

[1] BLEDISLOE, Charles Bathurst, 1st VISCOUNT, P.C., G.C.M.G., K.B.E., F.S.A., M.P. (Unionist) for South Wilts, 1910–18. Parliamentary Secretary to the Ministry of Food, 1916–17. Director of Sugar Distribution, 1917–19. Parliamentary Secretary to the Ministry of Agriculture, 1924–28. Governor-General of New Zealand, 1930–35.

years ago when we were both members of the Empire Marketing
Board, an organisation which I greatly deplore has disappeared.
On those occasions, curiously enough, I represented the farmers
of England and Wales : he of course quite rightly represented
the producing interests of his own great country, Australia. I
do not think that we always entirely agreed, but I noticed that
he did agree when I ventured to say at the first meeting of the
Marketing Board that I attended, " Please remember that little
England is an integral part of the British Empire." However,
since those days I feel sure that I have developed a less insular
outlook, and I am perfectly certain after listening to Mr.
McDougall's speech to-day that he himself has done likewise.

What I want to venture to urge is that we do not rest content
with Conferences. I seem to have attended many Conferences
of a similar character during the last thirty years, which have
in their result produced extremely little. Surely the time has
come when conferences, particularly at this real crisis in international affairs and for the future destinies of the British
Empire, must eventuate in action, and action, so far as we are
concerned, that is corporate and mutually sympathetic between
different parts of the British Empire, based upon knowledge.

If there is one thing more than another that has come home
to me since I left New Zealand, where I had the honour of
representing his late Majesty, King George V, for five years, it
is the appalling ignorance of the average Englishman, Scots-
man and Welshman—not to mention the Irishman—about the
British Empire, and of the outlook and policy of other nations
in the British Commonwealth besides ourselves.

The Chairman referred to the Statute of Westminster. I am
not sure that Australia is very keen about the Statute of
Westminster : I am quite certain that New Zealand is not, but
while emphasising the importance of recognising that under the
Statute of Westminster we have for all time recognised the
autonomy of the various self-governing parts of the British
Empire, do let us remember that they still look to the Mother
Country to give them a lead, and it is in so many matters the
absence of a definite lead on the part of the Mother Country and
her Government which eventuates in various difficulties with
which we feel ourselves confronted.

Sir Josiah Stamp used two expressions in his message to this

Conference which found a re-echo in my own heart—' Example '
and ' Initiative'. It is up to us as the predominant partner in
the British Commonwealth to provide example and initiative.
He went on to stress the value of the stability of the British
Empire as the foundation of world peace and prosperity.

I do not want to take up too much of your time, but I should
like to refer to the relative importance of production and
consumption. When we speak of consumption as a factor that
we have to consider in our Empire economics as of at least
equal importance to production, let us bear in mind that so
far as our home market is concerned, the British housewife is
an extremely particular person, and if you are going to develop
any policy of Empire preference or protection which is based
on anything other than the best and most uniform quality, I
am sure that it will prove a failure. In that sense I feel that
we must discriminate between competing food products of
varying quality and description. If you are going to put a
premium upon the less competent food producer by contrast
with the more competent food producer, in the long run you
will be up against the British consumer.

Mr. McDougall referred with great interest, and devoted a
good deal of his address to the unfortunately declining birth rate
in every country throughout the British Empire, but he
emphasised at the same time the declining death rate as a
result no doubt of improved hygienic conditions in certain
areas, and of better food. I was interested to hear him say that
the decreased death rate was not at the cost of the physical
stamina of the British race or of our people within the British
Commonwealth, and there passed through my mind the record
achievements of two great New Zealanders, Lovelock, in the
field of athletics, and Jean Batten in that of aviation. Mr.
McDougall pointed out by reference to vital statistics the
greater longevity of the average Britisher, but are vital statistics less important than natal statistics ? I want to see a
definite premium put upon the increased fertility of sound
British human beings, and I do not think, until we can counter
the excessive attractions of the motor-car, the cinema and the
other pleasurable diversions that he has mentioned, that we
shall ever solve this question of increasing the population of
the British Empire to the advantage of the whole Empire and

its greater security. Somehow or other a definite premium must be put upon the increased production of our race, children of the best possible type viewed both from the physical and mental standpoints. Two things more I should like to say. There is undoubtedly some difference of opinion, which is evidenced by our newspapers, about the advantages of the present negotiations between the United States and ourselves with a view to a happier economic relation between the two. Nothing delighted me more both in Sir Josiah Stamp's communication and in the address of our distinguished speaker than the fact that they emphasised the enormous importance to the British Empire and to its economic advancement of entering into happier trading relations with the other great section of the British race, the United States of America.

The last matter that I want to refer to is this. Increased output of agricultural produce and an incentive supplied by Government policy in producing an increased output, do not necessarily mean the increased prosperity of the farmer. Somehow or other the reasonable margin of profit that ought to accrue to the producer is absorbed in transmission between the producer and the consumer. It is a problem facing every self-governing part of the British Empire to-day, as to how to give the producer of food a reasonable reward for his energy, enterprise and capital, and at the same time maintain a reasonably low level of price for food produce of high quality for our whole population. Until that problem is solved, I am blessed if I know how you are going to augment the supply of those fundamental foods upon which the nutrition of the British race is said to depend.

Sir HAL COLEBATCH[1]: Conferences, as the last speaker has reminded us, too often " lose themselves in a waste of words." What practical result is likely to come from a conference of this kind ? My own feeling is that the direction in which such conferences are most likely to be helpful is in the creating of a better understanding and a greater knowledge amongst our people of those parts of the Empire about which at present they know so little. Do not run away with the idea that it is only

[1] COLEBATCH, Hon. Sir Hal, C.M.G., Agent-General for Western Australia. Late Premier of Western Australia. Member of the Senate of the Commonwealth of Australia, 1928–33.

the English people who know nothing about the Empire. A
little while ago a visiting lady from Australia of exceptionally
good intelligence came to me in great distress and said that
someone in England had asked her whether Perth was the
capital of Victoria, and she was amazed and shocked at his
ignorance. I said to her, " What is the capital of Saskatche-
wan ? " and she replied, " There isn't such a place."

At a recent conference you may remember a Bishop made
reference to the condition of affairs prevailing in Canada, and
said that notices were stuck up inviting people to offer themselves for employment, but adding, " No Englishmen need
apply." I should hesitate to question the statement of a
Bishop, but on the following day I had a quarter of an hour's
conversation with a Canadian Bishop, and he ridiculed the
idea. He said something of the sort might have happened : an
eccentric individual might have stuck up such a notice, but to
suggest that this represented the idea of the Canadians towards
Englishmen, Scotsmen or Irishmen was absurd.

Some Australians come to me saying that English people
make them feel as though they regarded them as inferior beings.
One old lady in Australia, when invited by her son to make a
trip to England, rejected the offer with contempt and said,
" What, go to that horrible place where all the convicts came
from ? No ! "

I am quite sure of this, that if any Britisher goes to Australia
or any of the other Dominions and finds himself unwelcome, or
if any Australian comes to this country and has a similar feeling,
the fault lies with that individual. I speak as one who spent
the first seven years of his life in this country, who has spent
eight of the last fourteen years over here, and who in the
interval has lived for over fifty years in Australia. I know
something of the conditions on both sides.

I wish to congratulate Mr. McDougall on his excellent paper,
and I hope that his conversion to the principle of international
co-operation is complete. I do hope that none of us will merely
pay lip service to this idea. I hope that we shall recognise that
you cannot have international co-operation without very considerable sacrifice on our part. The United States and Great
Britain are the two richest countries in the world, and if there
is to be international co-operation, it is the rich countries that

have to give up something and make sacrifices. You cannot have international co-operation without that : you cannot even expect to get back, directly, as much as you give. When the wealthy countries are endeavouring to establish some form of world co-operation, they must recognise that they are the wealthy countries and must expect to give more than they get. I know that sectional interests have raised their heads against any idea of trade agreements with America, saying that such a thing may do harm to this industry or that, but I believe that unless something is done to establish some form of world co-operation we shall—and perhaps more quickly than we think—reach an economic crisis more severe than that which struck us in 1929, and perhaps a world crisis more disastrous than that that faced us in 1914. It is the alternative we have to consider, not the fear of losing something here or there, but the sure knowledge that unless we can re-establish world trade, understanding and co-operation, there must inevitably be a collapse of our civilisation.

There is one other point upon which I would like to touch. The speaker emphasised the necessity of producing the best possible human beings. I know there is a feeling abroad to-day that the young people growing up are not what we were, when we were young. I do not know whether it is true or not, but I do know that if it is true, the fault is not theirs but ours. I consider it a disgrace to this country and a disgrace to my own country, Australia, that we have not long ago recognised the necessity in this steadily altering and progressive world of increasing the standard of education of our children, making the compulsory age limit higher. As a matter of fact, we have lowered the standard because the apprenticeship system, which was a form of education, has almost disappeared.

Several of the Australian States say they would be glad to receive farm labourers, domestic workers and skilled artisans. There are upwards of a million unemployed in this country, but where can you get half a dozen of either of these classes ? A great deal of farm land lies idle because of the scarcity of labour : domestic servants are very difficult to get, and industry is suffering from the lack of skilled labourers. Since the War we have had up to two million unemployed : is it not a dreadful thing to think that we now have more than a million unemployed and that industries are unable to obtain satisfactory labour ? We have to face the question of the rising generation : we have to do the best we can for our children, and it can be done. Children from the lowest class of the population should have wider opportunities. A great man, once a pillar of St. Paul's, and now represented by two columns in the *Evening Standard*, once said that some people have the idea that genius only came from the poorer classes. " No advocate of better opportunities for the poor ever made any such suggestion." Good material comes from all classes. We cannot afford to waste any, and in the past we have been wasting it lamentably.

Why is it that during recent years there have been far more British people leaving Australia and coming here than have been leaving here for Australia ? The balance has been made up : we have preserved an excess of immigration over migration, by the aid of foreigners—chiefly southern Europeans. These people come without assistance from their own Government ; without promise of help from ours, and they do well. Why is it that British people are not going there ? Is it because Australia is a poor country ? From the end of the War until 1929 Australia was borrowing, chiefly in this country, something like forty million pounds per annum. It went out not in money but in goods—largely capital goods for development and increased production. In 1929 two things happened. The borrowing policy was cut off as with a knife, and from that day not one sixpence has been borrowed in this country excepting for conversion purposes. In 1929 all those products, on the increase of which our borrowings had been spent, dropped so much in price that not one was profitable to the producers. Had Australia not been a wonderfully rich country with an energetic and resourceful people, she must have collapsed under those conditions, but from that day to this we have not defaulted one sixpence of our external or internal debt. We have paid every penny : our credit stands high : our production is increased, and we shall be one of the first countries to bring our unemployment figures down to normal. Why is it that a country like that does not attract men and capital ? Don't cast the blame on the rank and file. It is the brain rather than the brawn that has failed. There is too great a disposition on the part of those who have wealth and education and should be leaders, to increase their wealth by speculation : often by the worst and least productive form of speculation such as the speculation in synthetic currencies. Germany, Italy and Japan are confronted with grave economic problems, and many wonder how they can do so much with so little money. Don't forget that they are not carrying the two loads. We carry—the idle rich at the top and the idle poor at the bottom. We as an Empire will not get out of our difficulties until we can re-establish at least something of the old spirit of the merchant adventurers who " carried the trade and commerce of England to the four corners of the earth, and in doing it placed the wide bounds of our Empire in the sunrise and the sunset."

Mr. MUNRO ROGER : I have had a good deal of experience in this question of Empire development. I would like to point out that, although this Conference is on Empire development it appears to be limited to the academic discussion of economic features.

With reference to the proposed American Trade Agreement— what is the object of that agreement ? Obviously that their advantages in trading with us shall be increased. What are we going to sacrifice ? We are perpetually expected to sacrifice. Sir Hal Colebatch has said that the wealthy nations must make sacrifices, but I would ask what are we wealthy in ? Colossal debts and distressed areas chiefly ! We have a capital debt of nearly £9,000,000,000 and an annual expenditure of nearly £900,000,000—fifty per cent more than our pre-War National Debt. We are the most heavily taxed nation in the world. Our industries are consequently seriously handicapped in the world's markets. Our population is threatened with a rapid decline, with momentous consequences. Are we really a wealthy Nation ? America already has a huge credit trading balance with us. Last trading year we bought £93,000,000 of goods from her, whilst she bought only £27,000,000 from us. Which of our Empire's industries are going to be sacrificed to give her more?

What do you see in the great foreign international alliance recently made ? The *Daily Telegraph* rightly saw in it a sinister significance—and I know they are right. I know the Continent well and knew that alliance or something like it was coming. I was in Rome before the Abyssinian War, and Italian friends told me it was coming. They also cautiously hinted at a combination to challenge the British Empire and its possessions. That combination has been achieved. I would advise you to read Miss Taskerville's new book on Mussolini and his ambitions—definitely affecting our Empire.

Lord Halifax goes to Germany, as Lord Haldane did before the Great War, with sanguine expectations of " patting the tiger on the back " and expecting him to be good, whilst his appetite is unsatisfied. The day after his return Hitler in a public speech warned us that if we do not do what they expect we shall see what we shall get within five years ! It has just been reported that Germany will by and by have 2,4000,000 military effectives and Mussolini's pet editor, Signor Gayda, boasts of 20,000,000 tons of warships between them. Japan has plainly declared many times her ambitions for her own people, and there is ample evidence that she intends to dominate the East and probably more. Her firm belief is that her Emperor is divine and that they are a people divinely destined to rule the world ! Are we going to be weak and make concessions blindly ? There is little doubt that that combination has the intention to challenge our right to maintain empty spaces and unused resources in our Empire. That may involve another hideous holocaust of the manhood of the Nation and Empire in resisting. Think of this, I beg of you, and be awake !

Mrs. LIONEL GOLDSMID : I only want to say one word in answer to the points touched on by Lord Bledisloe and Sir Hal Colebatch.

It is the question of population that is so vital to this Empire. You men need fear no decrease in our population if you will only assure us that there will be no war. It is not because we women want motor-cars and cinemas that the birth rate is declining, but it is because we refuse to produce what is nothing but cannon fodder. Do remember that, and try to make the Empire such that it and the world will be safe from war.

Lt.-Col. WALEY COHEN[1]: I only wish that some parts of Sir

---

[1] COHEN, Lt.-Col. Charles Waley, C.M.G. Member of Colonial Office Committee of Emigrants' Information Board, 1904–10. Member of the Farmers' Club.

Hal Colebatch's speech could have been broadcast to a larger audience, but there is one point which I hope he will think over before repeating it. He suggested that the increase of the education age would lead to our having a greater number of domestic servants, farm labourers and skilled artisans. I think that is wrong. I deplore with him the decay in apprenticeship, and I rather feel that we have to get a new outlook in our education system if we really want to solve what is this very serious problem in this country—the difficulty of getting skilled labourers and skilled artisans.

My old friend, Mr. McDougall, made, as he always makes, a most stimulating address. The centre point appears to me to be the question of the real density of population. The desert areas of Australia and the rugged mountains in other parts of the Empire must be omitted from our calculations, but we found in the past that a successful migration policy and increase in the standard of living was based on this—that whereas it required five or six hundred pounds of extra capital to put a family into earning power in England, in Canada or Australia only one hundred pounds of extra capital was needed before the War to put them into a really productive position.

Let me refer to housing. In congested urban areas improvement in housing costs nearly twice as much as in rural areas. To improve the standard is much more expensive as density increases, and it will be found that some of the faults Mr. McDougall puts down to nutrition really are due to density of population.

The real problem appears to be how economically can we transfer some of the capital from this country to the Dominions, and economically transfer some of the population as well. That is the root problem.

One of the reasons why I think the nutrition standard is so much higher in Australia and in New Zealand, as Mr. McDougall has said, is because they have a smaller density of population. Before the War that was borne out by the fact that whereas in New Zealand the bulk of the population was fairly evenly scattered over the country, in Australia it was much more congested in the large towns : the mortality and child welfare conditions before the War in New Zealand and Australia bear out my point.

One speaker has referred to the numbers of conferences that have taken place. I am appalled at the number of conferences I have attended from which little has come. I want some serious effort to be made to deal with this question of density of population and the economic problem of the transfer of capital so as to enable the less thickly populated parts of the British Empire to absorb those who come from this country.

May I draw one parallel. Heaven forbid that we should develop exactly like the United States. In 1933 and last year I did a small survey in parts of it, and there is no doubt that the balance of the population there is leading them to many difficult problems. But if the total increase of the development of the population between 1840 and 1920 in the United States is compared with that throughout the British Empire, one cannot help wondering at the contrast.

What I should like to see as the result of this Conference would be a Committee set up to work on this problem and try to develop a practical scheme to solve it.

Mr. A. A. SOMERVILLE[1]: May I refer at once to what was said by Mrs. Goldsmid. There is not the least doubt that she is perfectly right in saying that if the world were sure of peace, or, at any rate, if the British Empire were sure of peace, there would be an increase in fertility. There are two things that I believe would produce a rise in the birth rate : the assurance of peace in the world, and a prosperity producing a rise in the standard of living.

With regard to peace, I would say that if we want peace we must be strong enough to defend it, and it is satisfactory, so far as it goes, to feel that every day is adding to the power of the British Empire, and particularly of this country, to defend peace.

The Chairman referred to several very interesting points : he mentioned the Statute of Westminster. Some of us in the House of Commons would have preferred that that Statute had been passed in a somewhat different form, but it has made very little difference. The whole Empire knew before that every

---

[1] SOMERVILLE, Annesley Ashworth, J.P., V.D., M.P. (Conservative) for the Windsor Division of Berks since 1922. Assistant Master and Head of the Army Class, Eton College, 1885–1922. Member of Guildhall Conference on Imperial Migration, October, 1937.

part of the Empire was in effect perfectly free to follow its own destiny, but the Statute of Westminster made this legal. I believe that the result of greater freedom is greater unity, and I believe also that, in the case of the two countries in which there have been some indications of a desire to break loose, within twenty years' time, those indications will have disappeared, and that those countries will be as keen and as integral parts of the British Empire as Australia, New Zealand or Canada.

The Chairman has spoken of the Conference on Migration recently held in the Guildhall. The two Conferences are to a large extent complementary. The Conference at the Guildhall was in the nature of a popular appeal from the centre of the British Empire to the outer Empire to take in hand the question of development steadily, systematically and in a businesslike way, and in particular to urge the Government to set up efficient and adequate machinery with that end in view.

I would remind you that there was an Imperial Conference in 1911, and that that Conference recommended the setting up of a Royal Commission on Imperial Resources. This was set up in 1912, and it included some of the best men we had, presided over by Sir Edgar Vincent, later Lord d'Abernon, one of the members being Sir George Foster, together with leading representatives of life and thought in the Empire. That Commission sat for five years and did not content itself with sitting here ; it travelled over the Empire and got into contact with the leading men in the Empire. It reported in 1917. Unfortunately we were at a critical moment of the War then, and that report— a most valuable document which I would recommend all to read—dealt with the subject admirably and made weighty recommendations, but it was pigeon-holed, and nothing came of it until 1922, the date of the Empire Settlement Act. The main point of the report was this, that it looked upon the Empire as a great estate, owned by different members of the same family ; it used the expression ' estate ' and ' domain ', and said : " Let the members of this great family get together and develop it ". Looking at the international situation to-day, is there not a danger, very present, that other nations will say, " You have a great estate. A large part of that is undeveloped. You cannot develop it. Let us do it." We have to meet that, and therefore the question is pressing. There has not been an answer yet to the question of how to proceed to the systematic, businesslike, co-operative development of that great Society.

Sir Hal Colebatch spoke of the cutting off of loan money from this country after the War, and he asked us to look at the result, and the result was wholly good. Therefore the cutting off was a blessing in disguise. Australia, as a matter of fact, was top-heavy in the matter of loans : the amount of loan money per head of the population in Australia was dangerous. He is perfectly right in saying that no investment from this country in Australia has been in default, and personally I wish that the hundreds of millions of money invested in foreign countries were invested in the British Empire and devoted to its improvement. Australia having put her affairs in order, we want businesslike and systematic development in conjunction with Australia to develop the resources of the country. It is an immense subject.

Mr. McDougall spoke about the lack of proper distribution, and that is a great problem, here and throughout the Empire and the world. Why should we not have an Empire movement to diminish the cost of distribution ? That is a possibility. Mr. McDougall spoke of money as the lubricant of trade. There is plenty of capital lying idle. We have seen the rush of capital into Government securities and, lately, away from industry. We do not want that : it should be productively employed, and if this country and the Dominions will in conjunction co-operatively undertake the development of the great resources of the Empire, I believe the result would be the raising of the standard of living all through the Empire, the return to prosperity, the rise of the birth rate and therefore greater power of defence and greater international trade. The British Empire cannot be prosperous without to a large extent making the rest of the world prosperous also.

There are two great tendencies in the world to-day, and they are becoming more and more opposed—democracy and dictatorship—and dictatorship is saying to democracy, " You have great possessions, the British Empire in particular. You are not developing them as you might. Give us an opportunity or we will take it." Democracy has to meet that challenge and prove that, as represented by the British Empire, she can meet it, and the result will be prosperity for the Empire and for the world.

Sir ARTHUR AITON[1]: I would like to say a few words particularly addressed to the ignorance that is present not only in the Empire, and not only in this end of the Empire, because I remember my daughter was for a year at a scholastic establishment in the United States, where she was asked by a young woman whether they kept Christmas in England!

I can claim to know something about the Empire; I was born in the East, I have visited every section of the Empire except Newfoundland, and I have also visited many other parts of the world. I have found a tremendous amount of ignorance within the Empire concerning the rest of the world. In this respect I have had it put to me in South Africa whether I did not consider that it was a wonderful agricultural country. I had only to think of the Argentine, which is *really* a wonderful agricultural country. When discussing these matters of Empire, we must remember that there are other parts of the world which are equally, if not better, fitted to produce the food of the world than many parts of the Empire.

Education is a most difficult subject. I have made some endeavour to get the History of the Empire introduced into our educational system. My experience so far is, that on going to Westminster I was told that it is a matter dealt with by the Local Authorities, whereas the Local Authorities said that it is a matter to be left to the whim of the various teachers, with the result that nothing is done. A meeting of this sort could do some good if everyone present would make it their business to press that the education of this country should include the History of the British Empire. The primary educationalists are not the only sinners, because the Public Schools are equally bad. When my son was at school, I was told that geography was not education, and was only taught to boys who had not enough brains to learn anything else.

As to the undeveloped parts of the Empire, I do not believe there are many. Australia has a great many parts not inhabited, but that does not say that they are undeveloped. On looking at the map you can see miles of undeveloped country, but to get

[1] AITON, Sir Arthur, C.B.E., 1918. Governing Director of Aiton and Co., Ltd., Derby and other companies.

migration into that country is exceedingly difficult owing to climatic conditions. One also comes up against the feeling of the Trade Unions growing up in the Dominions, that if we are going to send out skilled men they will flood the market and lower the standard of living.

Reverting to Australia and New Zealand, we came to the conclusion that it was useless to try to do anything at present, while there are such large numbers of unemployed.

I wish to thank Mr. McDougall for the address he has given. He comes from Australia, but he has a very good-sounding name, and he is an instance of what can be done in the Empire by distributing as many of such good-sounding names as possible throughout the length and breadth of it.

Mr. B. O. SCHONEGEVEL[1]: I listened with great interest to what was so ably said by Mr. McDougall, who I did not realise was an Australian. The only reference I found made to South Africa was made by a speaker who said we were a very poor agricultural country. But we were told this morning that gold was a lubricant. It is true that people in England are not sufficiently conversant with the opportunities that exist beyond the confines of the old country. To me, as a South African, and a Dutch South African, the Empire is like the human frame. The most vital part is the heart, and the limbs and body are complementary to the heart, and so it behoves us all to continue to develop the muscles in the tail of the kangaroo and the legs of the springbok. We must take care, however, in our anxiety to develop the muscles, that we do not strain the heart, for it is the heart, after all, which gives the life to the body. I welcome the Statute of Westminster because it gives responsibility to the Dominions. If they want to be independent, then let them realise that independence brings responsibility. I believe that the Dominions are fully prepared to take responsibility, and indeed we see that they are, all of them, now developing their armaments energetically.

As a one time leader of a political party in South Africa, whenever a worthy man became irresponsible, I gave him a job and the responsibility at once sobered him.

[1] SCHONEGEVEL, B. O. Mayor of Kingwilliamstown, Cape Province, South Africa. Member of the Assembly of the Cape Province, Union of South Africa.
D

With regard to the Colonies, South Africa is not holding on to the former German Colony of South-West Africa because of the great value of that country, for, as a matter of fact, as a country it is of little consequence save from the point of view of protection. We stand for PEACE. We in the Union want no war, and we shall not be prepared to bring on to our borders again a neighbour who might cause trouble in the future.

Dr. DRUMMOND SHIELS[1]: I think you will agree that the Royal Empire Society has done well in summoning this Conference. It is carrying out one of the main objectives of the Society by getting down to the study of problems which vitally affect the welfare of the Empire, and in an atmosphere more objective and scientific that is possible when these matters are discussed in the clash of party politics.

Like Lord Bledisloe, I had the privilege of being a colleague of Mr. McDougall on the Empire Marketing Board. I knew we should get something good to-day, and we have all—I am sure —admired his technical ability and the fine broad spirit in which he has addressed himself to these important problems.

With regard to the population question, I believe that the gloomy prognostications of statisticians would be less likely to be fulfilled if something of what Mr. McDougall has set before us could be carried out. One reason for the low birth rate, not sufficiently realised, is the economic factor. People want a high standard for their children, physically and educationally, and do not wish to go beyond their economic resources. What Mrs. Goldsmid said about the effect of the fear of war, also, is undoubtedly true.

It is, perhaps, rather misleading to speak about the improvement in the average expectation of life. It is true that this has considerably increased in the last century, but the actual span of life itself has not increased, and, indeed, there are many who believe that the rush, excitement and strain of modern conditions are tending to reduce the length of that span. Anything, therefore, which would help to increase the sense of economic and other security would tend to better health and longer life.

[1] SHIELS, T. Drummond, M.C., M.B., Ch.B. (Edin.), Fellow and ex-President of the Royal Medical Society. M.P. (Labour) for East Edinburgh, 1924–31. Parliamentary Under-Secretary of State for India, 1929. Parliamentary Under-Secretary of State for the Colonies, 1929–31.

Mr. McDougall spoke wisely of the importance of increasing the standard of life throughout the British Empire and of relating its resulting prosperity to the welfare of the whole world. We have the scientific knowledge to enable us to bring this about, but we are not applying it.

The difficulty under the present system is that greater efficiency in production brings immediate unemployment, and although it is true that there is a vast capacity for increased consumption, there is no automatic adjustment of supply to need, and so we have chronic unemployment, made better or worse by almost regular cycles. But much of what Mr. McDougall suggests could be carried out with advantage even with our present economic arrangements.

With regard to migration, while one should not regret the going of citizens of other countries into any one of our Dominions, one can only hope that the reason they are going in such numbers into Canada, for example, is not because they are willing to put up with a lower standard of life than British citizens. That would be unfortunate from the point of view of the general thesis which Mr. McDougall has set before us.

The speech of Sir Hal Colebatch breathed a fine spirit, not only of democracy, but also of a vigorous belief in the essentials of Mr. McDougall's programme. He and others have pointed out that the remedies required for solving these problems would create political difficulties.

While that is true, I believe there is far more common ground in all parties than we realise, and more public goodwill that could be mobilised towards a solution than has yet been secured.

The raising of the standard of life for the whole Empire, with its beneficial reactions on the rest of the world, is a great objective. It is true—as Mr. McDougall pointed out—that whenever proposals are put forward for raising the standard of life of the people, whether with regard to nutrition, housing, education or anything else, sectional interests rise up and proclaim good reasons why it should not be attempted. There is no doubt, however, that the improvement in the standard of life in this country, and still more in India and the Colonies, is proceeding at too slow a pace, and large sections of our various people are not sharing in it at all. We ought to get ahead on our common ground, so far as it will take us ; and I think it will be found that anything which is more humane, more kindly and just, anything which improves the health and the social life of our widespread peoples will be found in the end to be truly economic. The Royal Empire Society should proceed along the lines started in this Conference, and thereby it may be privileged to make a useful contribution towards the objective so admirably set before us in this session of the Conference.

Mr. CHARLES H. LUKE : I happened some time ago to be with a diplomatist who knew all the Chancelleries of Europe and I asked what was the effect on the world of the fifteen hundred million pound resolution to improve our defences put before the House of Commons by Mr. Chamberlain, and the reply was, " They are scared stiff in all parts of the world."

Do you not think that if some of the suggestions put forward this morning with regard to the development of our estate were put before the House of Commons by a resolution that five or six hundred millions be spent in co-operation with the Dominions on developing the territories of the Empire, that the world would be quieted down, and not scared stiff, because they would know that we were determined to have peace ? We shall never get peace by arming every part of the Empire, but we shall if we develop our estate.

Fifty years ago in Canada it was stated by public writers that Canada could support, on an agricultural basis, 150 millions of people, and that I believe is still true. It is a great failure of our governmental powers in all parts of the Empire that we have not been able to solve that difficulty in the last fifty years. We must get the Dominions to agree with us to improve our development.

Sir ARCHIBALD WEIGALL : May I be allowed to make some comments on the subjects that have been referred to, from the point of view simply of the Royal Empire Society and what it is trying to do.

Mr. Somerville and Lieut.-Colonel Waley Cohen are seized with the idea that we must get this family estate really going. I want for one moment to ask them in practice how that is to be done with the Statute of Westminster on the Statute Book ? It is necessary to realise the relationship between Federal Governments and this Government, and still far more important, the relationship between the State Governments in Australia and the Federal Government. Unless and until we can persuade, rightly or wrongly, the electorate in those States, we shall not get one yard further. With a Government sitting for only three years, with an eye on the ballot-box, it is impossible to get the idea over unless and until the electorate is persuaded.

Three years ago it was my privilege to go to Australia, and the Broadcasting people were kind enough to arrange for me to talk to the whole of Australia. As I said at the Guildhall at the Conference on Migration, which has already been mentioned, the practical thing is for young men, Members of Parliament, who are equipped with a certain amount of knowledge of Australia from here, to go there, not as lecturers or dictators, but as brothers belonging to the same estate, and try to put that over. That is the practical way of dealing with the problem.

I think Mr. McDougall's paper was most admirable, because within three-quarters of an hour he covered the whole of the development for the next century. He had hitched his wagon to a very high star and visualised a complete Utopia, because he said that what had to be done was to get all within the Empire to regard it as a whole, and not to dwell on any particular section. Do not let us be too excited or enthusiastic about this, because human nature changes very slowly. For instance, it will be a long time before Australian capitalists will sit down and say, " We are going to look at this from the point of view of the British Empire. Blow Australia ! Blow our State ! "

I am very glad to see present two very distinguished members of the farming community in this audience. I was very interested to hear Mr. McDougall say that in comparing production and costs of distribution we were putting a premium on inefficiency. Lord Bledisloe agreed. But there is another side : if all the affairs of life were ruled entirely by the head, we should not be half as happy.

My profession was that of an agricultural agent before I was lured to the less profitable paths of public life, and I was a Resident Agent on 50,000 acres in this country. I so well remember being very enthusiastic in my work, and I went to the great territorial magnate who owned the land and spoke to him about one of his tenants, and said : " We have had no rent from this fellow for two years ; he is a hopeless farmer, a thoroughly good fellow, but really inefficient." He looked at me in amazement and said, " What, get rid of old So-and-so ? Never ! He taught me to shoot ! " That kind of thing all makes life very happy, but perhaps not efficient. None the less, I feel we are under an enormous debt of gratitude to our speaker this morning for his admirable address. We could not have had a better send-off for our first great Conference in this new building than we have had this morning. I hope Mr. McDougall will accept our heartfelt thanks.

REPLY

Mr. McDougall : There are one or two things I would like to say in commenting on some of the points made. First and foremost I must correct a most serious misapprehension under which the Chairman is labouring. He has inferred that I have suggested that the Federal or State Governments of Australia might be expected to say : "We have to think of the whole Empire and agree to a policy beneficial to the whole Empire, even if detrimental to Australia." Nothing could be further from anything I have ever had in my mind. The suggestion I am putting forward is that in each part of the Empire instead of our being so concerned about the particular interests of sections of producers, we should take a broad line, and in each part of the Empire regard the raising of the general standard of the whole of our own populations as being our first objective. In order to do that it will prove necessary to bring about certain measures of collaboration between Empire countries and also foreign countries.

A sound point was raised by Mrs. Goldsmid. She asked that the Governments of the Empire should take such action as would result in keeping the Empire at peace. Of course there is no Government of the Empire that is not anxious to do so, but frankly it is impossible for the British Empire, even acting together, to guarantee peace in the world. We may be able to keep the British Empire out of war, but even that is far from sure, and I would suggest that one of the best possible ways of insuring peace—though perhaps a long-range method—is to develop to the fullest possible extent this general ideal of economic appeasement and better standards of living. There

is no nation at the present moment following the path of actual
or potential aggression which is not also finding the standard
of living of its people falling. If the agressively minded nations
can be shown how other nations are improving their standards
of living, and if we are always ready to offer to all nations the
fullest possible economic co-operation, I think that along those
lines there is the greatest hope of peace.

Colonel Waley Cohen suggested that density of population
was probably one of the biggest factors affecting mortality
rates. I wonder if he is right, or if he has ever made a study
of two districts in the United States. Manhattan Island is the
most densely populated area in the world, but if he studies the
vital statistics of that island and of Tennessee, he will, I think,
come to the conclusion that ignorance and poverty are perhaps
more violent destroying agencies to human life than density of
population.

A number of speakers have mentioned the subject of migration. Is it not clear that all the difficulties we meet when we
start to think of how to arrange the redistribution of the
Empire's population might be more easily overcome if we took
more interest in these problems of increased consumption and
more efficient production, and brought them to the point when
they resulted in the improvement of the standard of living ?
From that we should find the way to a renewed migration
within the Empire far greater than it is to-day.

II

INDIA AND THE PROBLEM

Tuesday, November 23rd. Afternoon Session

SIR FIROZKHAN NOON,[1] High Commissioner for India, took the Chair.

SIR FIROZKHAN NOON: It is my pleasant duty to introduce to you Sir Frank Noyce. I think most of you know that he has just retired from India, where he held the highest appointment that any civilian can hold, as he was the Executive Counsellor to His Excellency the Viceroy. It is my great pleasure to be associated with him to-day because I count him as one of my oldest friends. I have met him in Simla for many years, and have known him intimately. I can say without fear of contradiction that there can be no civilian who has left more sincere friends in India than Sir Frank Noyce.

Throughout his tenure of office, Sir Frank Noyce showed deep sympathy for Indian aspirations and Indian needs. He won the confidence of all Indians with whom he came in contact not only inside the Legislature, where he worked so well, but outside also, and it is particularly fortunate that at this Session of the Conference we should have a man of his administrative experience, learning, and Indian sympathies, who places before us some aspects of India as connected with the rest of the Empire.

SIR FRANK NOYCE[2]: I imagine that everyone of those who have been called upon to open the discussions at the Sessions of this Conference thinks that he has had the most difficult task

[1] NOON, Hon. Malik Sir Firozkhan. High Commissioner for India. Member of the Legislative Council, Punjab, 1921–37. Minister for Public Health, Punjab, 1927–31. Minister for Education, Punjab, 1931–37.
[2] NOYCE, Sir Frank, K.C.S.I., C.B.E., late I.C.S. Member of the Executive Council of the Governor-General of India in charge of the Industries and Labour Department, 1932–36. Secretary of the Government of India Department of Education, Health and Lands, 1929–32. President of the Indian Coal Committee, 1924. President of the Indian Tariff Board (Cotton Textile Industry Enquiry), 1926.

assigned to him. I put forward my claim to that onerous distinction without any hesitation for two reasons. The first is a personal one. The invitation to speak to-day reached me almost simultaneously with the news of a very serious climbing accident to my elder son. My preoccupations with that have prevented my devoting to the preparation of my speech the attention the importance of the subject deserves and must be my excuse for some of, though by no means all, its imperfections.

My second reason is the vastness of India. Before I go any further, I should perhaps explain that no speaker for India is now entitled to speak for Burma, which, from April 1st last, ceased to be a part of the Indian Empire. Separate statistics for Burma are not, however, at present available, at any rate to me, and it is, therefore, impossible to exclude Burma from my purview this afternoon. There is the less need to do so because, although Burma, when a province of the Indian Empire, accounted for nearly one-eighth of the area of that Empire—233,500 square miles out of a total of 1,809,000 square miles—it only accounted for a little over 4 per cent of its population—14.5 millions against 353 millions, which, it may be noted in passing, is one-fifth of that of the whole world. Such figures as I shall give you are, therefore, only slightly affected by the separation of Burma.

And now for the background. No one here needs to be reminded that India is a predominantly agricultural country, the population of which is increasing at a rate which is enough, in itself, to give rise to serious problems in the near future. Between 1921 and 1931, the total population of India increased from 319 to 352.8 millions, that is by 10.6 per cent. It is true that the rate of increase in the urban population was 20 per cent against 9.6 per cent for the rural, but, as the latter in 1931 numbered 314 millions against only 39 millions for the former, the predominance of the rural population was only slightly affected. In the last fifty years, the total population of India has increaed by 39 per cent. The Public Health Commissioner for India, Colonel Russell, in his recent annual report, estimated that at the next census it will be found to have reached 400 millions. Put it in another way. Between 1921 and 1931, India added to herself the equivalent of the whole population of France or Italy.

Of India's 352 millions, 11 per cent only are classed as urban and 89 per cent as rural. That 89 per cent lives in 700,000 villages, the average population of each being about 450. Over 40 per cent of the rural population lives in villages of under 500 inhabitants and about 45 per cent in villages with populations between 500 and 2,000.

It will be obvious, therefore, that, nowhere in the Empire is that immense scope for increased demand for food, clothing, houses and for every sort of manufactured goods, which is stressed in the General Note on the aims and objects of this Conference,[1] as great as it is in India. Even if we were not dealing with such a vast population, that would still be true, for, as everyone who knows India is only too painfully aware, nowhere in the Empire is it more desirable that the standards of living should be raised than it is in India. Let me take the enormous unsatisfied needs in the order in which they are stated in the Note and deal first with food, from every point of view the most important in a country in which so large a proportion of the population is undoubtedly under-nourished, even if it is somewhat an exaggeration to state that it does not get one proper meal a day. Here let me offer a word of warning. I have little confidence in the various estimates which have been framed from time to time of the gross food supply in India as compared with the requirements of the population. In the first place, the statistics of production are far too incomplete, and under-estimates of the out-turn of crops—owing to the ingrained pessimism of the India reporting agency—far too common to admit of any great reliance being placed upon them. In the second place, every serious student of nutrition problems in villages has noticed that there are many useful foodstuffs, especially vegetables, which make little or no appearance in the crop returns, but which are, none the less, of very real importance. Equally with the estimates of gross food supply, it is, in my view, unsafe to trust the attempts which have been made to calculate the equivalent in calories of that supply, and to compare the result with what is required for a healthy population. Not only are many fundamental data on the composition and digestibility of India foodstuffs lacking, but we have, as yet, no proper figures of the requirements of an Asiatic popula-

[1] See Introduction.

tion living under tropical conditions. I said " as yet ", for with eminent experts like Dr. Aykroyd, the Director of Nutrition Research in India, working in this field, it should not be long before some of the lacunæ in this direction are filled in.

But, whatever the accuracy of the estimates, the fact remains incontrovertible that the yields of Indian agriculture are low, that, consequently, the villages remain poor and that the diet provided is almost entirely grain, is lacking in variety and is poor in animal products. It has been argued that a dangerous position is arising because, while the population is increasing, the area under food grains is not.

The official figures, as they stand, lend some support to this view. During the period 1908-9 to 1917-18, 0.89 acres per head of population were devoted to food crops, whilst during the period 1928-29 to 1932-33, the acreage had sunk to 0.79 per head. The population had increased by 28.7 millions, but the area under food crops had only gone up by 26 million acres, that is by 0.09 acres per head. The non-food crops, on the other hand, had kept pace with the population, the acreage per head being 0.044 in the earlier and 0.057 in the later of the two periods. It would, in my view, be dangerous to draw from these figures the inference which has been drawn from them by some that the villager has less food than he used to have. The more correct inference is, I think, that yields have increased. It would not be very creditable to the work the Agricultural Departments have done since the beginning of the century if this were not so. The main reason for the under-nourishment of so large a proportion of the Indian population is to be found elsewhere. It lies in the fact that, even when allowance is made for the foodstuffs which do not appear in the crop returns, so high a proportion of the food crops grown in India consists of grain crops. It is the quality, even more than the quantity, of the Indian dietary that is wrong. But it is not the quality of the food crops the Indian peasantry consumes that needs attention. Early this year, Sir John Russell, the Director of the Rothamsted Experimental Station, and Dr. Norman Wright, the Director of the Hannah Dairy Research Institute, Kirkhill, Ayr, both very eminent experts in their particular lines, went out to India to review the work of the Imperial Council of Agricultural Research. Their most valuable reports, which have recently been published and which I have found of the greatest assistance in preparing this paper, throw much light on this question. Sir John Russell's view, which can, I think, be accepted without hesitation, is that in dealing with food crops intended for home consumption, the Indian agriculturist should aim at securing the largest and healthiest crops possible, but need not concern himself with trying to change their composition. The amount of alteration possible is too small to justify the expenditure of time and resources that can better be spent in other ways.

The view that the India dietary is deficient in quality more than in quantity has been well illustrated by Dr. Aykroyd in two tables he has drawn up showing two dietaries—a common ill-balanced one and a well-balanced diet which should be substituted for it. The common ill-balanced diet consists of 20 ounces of cereals per day and only 7½ ounces of pulses, vegetables, fats and oils and milk. Fruit does not appear in it at all. In the well-balanced diet, cereals fall to 15 ounces ; pulses, vegetables, fats and oils, fruit and milk account for 25 ounces. It is the lack or insufficiency of the latter elements that accounts for the prevalence of ' deficiency diseases ' in India ; keratomolacia caused by deficiency of Vitamin A ; stomatitis caused by deficiency of Vitamin B ; low hæmoglobin content caused by iron deficiency, and so on. It is in respect of milk that the defects of the ill-balanced diet are specially apparent. In Dr. Aykroyd's well-balanced diet, the consumption of milk jumps to 8 ounces from the 2 ounces in the ill-balanced one. Dr. Wright goes much further than Dr. Aykroyd. Working on Dr. Aykroyd's material, he urges that the standard Indian requirement should be 15 ounces of milk per day against a standard European requirement of 35 ounces. Even 15 ounces a day is still double the quantity which he estimates as at present available in the country, namely 7 to 8 ounces per head. He points out that the standard Indian requirement would appear to have been somewhat arbitrarily fixed at a low figure to make it a feasible standard under Indian conditions. If the standard were to be fixed at a level more nearly akin to that aimed at in prosperous European countries, the present output of milk in India would not merely need to be doubled, but would have to be increased threefold to even fourfold.

How are the deficiencies in the India dietary to be set right ? How is the population—mainly, I need hardly remind you, a vegetarian population—to get the vegetables, fruit and protective foods, milk, ghee (clarified butter) and fats generally, of which it stands in such great need ? Here we are at once in real earnest up against the question of improving its purchasing power of which we always—and very rightly—hear so much in this and other connections, and for which it is so difficult to find a satisfactory and feasible solution. But in this matter of purchasing power, as Sir George Schuster pointed out in the deeply interesting Birdwood Lecture he delivered to the Royal Society of Arts in 1935, it is easy to exaggerate the difficulties, " After all," as he went on to say, " what is involved is no more than a process of exchange. Every seller becomes, *ipso facto*, a potential buyer. If A produces more milk and B produces more grain—in the light of what I have said, it would perhaps be more correct to say more vegetables, fruit and fodder crops —their positions fit in together, for A and his cows can consume more of B's foodstuffs, while B and his family can in exchange, consume more of A's milk and ghee and butter." What is needed is somehow or other to get the rural masses—and to a less degree, of course, the urban masses—out of the rut of their present low standards of living. Much can be done, as no one has realised more keenly than the present Viceroy, by education, propaganda and a reasonable measure of public assistance. But supposing an effective demand for a change in the Indian dietary—and more especially an effective demand for more milk—were aroused in this way, it may be asked where the land on which to grow the special foodstuffs is to come from?

I may say at once that I do not think that much assistance can be looked for from those millions of acres shown in the *Agricultural Statistics of India* as " Culturable waste other than fallow." As the Royal Commission on Agriculture in India, of which the present Viceroy was Chairman, said in their Report of 1928 when pressing for a re-examination of the figures under this head—which, so far as I know, has not yet been undertaken —it is certain that much of this area amounting to 152 million acres—an area which must have been very largely reduced by the separation of Burma—or nearly 23 per cent of the total area of British India could, in no conceivable circumstances, be brought under tillage. If such lands are accessible, they must be of the poorest quality or they would have been brought under cultivation long ago. If they are not accessible, they obviously cannot be cultivated. If we assume with Dr. Aykroyd, that at present the cultivator eats more cereals than he really needs, then some of the land devoted to cereals at present could be diverted to special food products. But even if pressure of population necessitated that all the land devoted to food grains should continue to be so used, there are other ways of dealing, at any rate partially, with the problem. What is needed is a better planning of the cropping of villages. Without very gravely disturbing the general balance of cash and food crops, there is undoubtedly scope for systems of cropping which would gradually improve the nutrition of the cultivator and of his cattle and raise the fertility of the soil. One way in which the present vicious circle might be broken would be to take fuller advantage of the fact that there are now in India at least twenty million acres under improved strains of crops, mostly cash crops, cotton, sugar cane and jute, all yielding, even at the most modest estimate, some 10 to 15 per cent more on the average than the varieties they have displaced.

Cotton, sugar cane and jute all present their special problems of which I shall have more to say later, but a study of those problems shows, I think, the undesirability of increasing the gross production of the cash crops by such a percentage as that I have just mentioned. That being so, the better course would appear to be to set free a portion of the land now devoted to cash crops and to utilise it for the cultivation of special food-stuffs. If the supply of milk is to be increased, it is essential that there should be a very much larger production of fodder crops, especially leguminous crops for both working and milch cattle. A beginning has been made with early maize and irrigated berseem (Egyptian clover) in what, after the area under the Lloyd Barrage in Sind, is the most important addition to the area under irrigation in India in recent years—the area irrigated by tube wells in the United Provinces for which those Provinces are largely indebted to the genius and enthusiasm of Sir William Stampe. It is only in ways such as this that one can hope to increase the supply of milk and ghee in the villages. Opportunities of doing so to some extent occur where schemes are in operation to remedy that curse of Indian agriculture, the fragmentation of holdings. India is essentially a country of small holdings. A special enquiry undertaken in 2,400 villages in the Punjab a few years ago showed that 18 per cent of the owner's holdings were under one acre, 25 per cent were between one and three acres, 15 per cent were between three and five acres and a further 18 per cent were between five and ten acres. And these figures would be on the high side for India as a whole, for the number of cultivated acres per cultivator in the Punjab is about nine, which is three times as much as it is in the United Provinces, Bengal or Bihar. Dr. Wright comments feelingly on the difficulties this presents to the establishment of a dairy industry. But worse remains. For those holdings, small as they are, are not solid blocks. If a father dies owning three isolated fields of one acre each and leaving three sons, the sons do not take one field each but one third of each field. Efforts are being made to secure the realignment of holdings. These have met with some success, notably in the Punjab. Apart from other advantages, they enable untidy corners to be turned into quite useful fodder plots.

It should, I think, be once again emphasised that whilst there is practically general agreement that the dietary of the greater part of the population in India is unsatisfactory both in quality and quantity, the data at present available are quite insufficient to enable the deficiencies in both respects to be determined with anything like exactitude. It would be a mistake, in this as in so many other respects, to generalise for the whole of India. Nutritional deficiencies have been studied more fully in Madras than elsewhere, but what is true for Madras may be regarded as holding good for most of the south and east of India, Bombay, Bihar, Orissa and the Central Provinces. In the Punjab and the United Provinces more wheat and milk— and in the Punjab with its very large Muslim and Sikh population more meat—are consumed and the problems are, therefore, rather different.

Everywhere, however, more study is required, and it is to be hoped that the recommendation made both by Sir John Russell and the Nutrition Advisory Committee of the India Research Food Association will be accepted. They propose that there should be a nutrition survey in each Province in order to discover the chief deficiencies revealed in the Indian dietary, after which the ways in which they can be put right would be determined by consultation between the agricultural and medical authorities. One important step which has recently been taken has been the appointment of a Nutrition Officer at Delhi to act as a Liaison Officer between the Nutrition Laboratory at Coonoor in South India and the Agricultural Research Institutes at Delhi and in the Provinces.

I have so far dealt with the improvement of India agriculture mainly from the point of view of nutrition. The scope for improvement generally is, of course, immense. Sir John Russell, dotting the i's and crossing the t's of that very voluminous document, the *Report of the Royal Commission on Agriculture*, has succinctly summed up the seven great factors capable of improving the yield of crops in India. They are better varieties of crops, better control of pests and diseases, better control of water supply for crops, the prevention of soil erosion, better use of manures and fertilisers, better implements and cultivations, and better systems of cropping—in particular, better rotations and the use of more fodder crops with the object of obtaining more farmyard manure. Much has been done in all these directions since the Royal Commission on Agriculture reported in 1928 and since the Imperial Council of Agricultural Research, the most important outcome of its labours, was established in 1929, but very much remains to be done. It is, however, good to find that Sir John Russell and Dr. Wright have given the work of the Imperial Council of Agricultural Research their very warm approval, qualified only by recommendations for its expansion in several important directions.

I have endeavoured to show, however sketchily—and I ought, I know, to have said more about the improvement of the cattle of India which constitute more than one third of cattle population of the world—the immense scope there is for increased efficiency of production in the broadest sense to India's most important industry, agriculture. But increased production from the soil of India is not in itself sufficient to secure a happy and contented countryside. An improvement in the standard of living in the purely material sense is only a partial solution of the problem. No efforts to improve agriculture will yield the fullest results unless village life is made more attractive and the villages are made fit to live in. The drift to the towns must be arrested, and the most strenuous endeavours must be made to keep on the land or to send back to it some of those thousands of young men who in recent years have swelled the army of educated unemployed to disquieting dimensions and have made the question of middle-class unemployment one of the two questions on the solution of which, it is not exaggerating greatly to say, depends in very large measure the future of India. The other is, of course, the communal question. Various colonisation and settlement experiments have been tried in the Punjab, the United Provinces and elsewhere, but it cannot be said that they have done more than touch the fringe of the problem. Much water has flown down the rivers of India since I left that country in April last after thirty-four and a half years of service to it, and I doubt whether any year in India has shown greater changes than 1937. But it is heartening to those interested in Indian village welfare—and who that knows India is not ?— that the new Provincial governments, whatever their composition, have without exception placed the improvement of Indian village life in the forefront of their programmes. The world offers no fairer field for the exercise of wisely directed enthusiasm, and it may be doubted whether anything would have a more far reaching effect on the prosperity of the Empire as a whole than the general raising of the standard of life in the Indian countryside.

I may well be told at this stage that I have dwelt too exclusively on the internal economy of India and on the need for greater production and consumption by the Indian people of their own products. Where, I shall be asked, does the Empire come in ? The answer to that question is contained, in the main, in the Introduction on the aims and objects of this Conference to which I have already referred. There, it is stated that increased consumption is dependent on increased purchasing power, which again is dependent upon enlarging the real national income of every portion of the Empire. In India, far the most potent way of enlarging the real national income is by improving agriculture upon which the improvement of that vital national asset, the health and morale of its people, must most largely depend. As Colonel Russell emphasises, the malnutrition of a very large proportion of the population of

E

India not only affects the mental and physical energy of the individual, but increases the morbidity and mortality of the many infectious diseases to which the ordinary individual is subjected in that country. That improvement of health and morale is, in its turn, bound to create enormous unsatisfied needs which the rest of the Empire can help to satisfy.

Before I pass on to the industrial aspect, I should like to say a few words about the cash crops, the exports of which are of such great importance to India. For it is on those exports that India mainly relies to meet not only the cost of her imports but also her home charges, military and civil, payment of pensions, leave salaries, payment of interest on loans, and the like, and, as Sir George Schuster emphasised in his lecture, it is the exported portion of the crop which makes all the difference to the general body of cultivators while, in those special areas which concentrate on growing crops like cotton, jute, tobacco, oilseeds and tea, the loss of export markets would, for the time being, at any rate, mean the destruction of the bulk of the people's livelihood. They are specially worthy of mention to-day, as some of them supply noteworthy instances of co-operation between different parts of the Empire, which it is the special object of this Conference to assist in fostering. The most striking instance of that co-operation has been furnished by the Lancashire Indian Cotton Committee, established in 1932 as the result of the discussions at the Ottawa Conference of that year on the development of trade between the nations of the British Commonwealth. The Committee has, I may perhaps remind you, two main lines of activity. It has a Commissioner in India who works in close co-operation with the Indian Central Cotton Committee, a most capable and efficient body for whose establishment I am proud to think that, as Secretary of the Indian Cotton Committee of 1917–18, I was in some degree responsible, and also with the Provincial Agricultural Departments, in promoting the production and preparation for the market of more and more of the types of cotton which Lancashire can use. It also conducts a most thorough programme of research and experiment in Lancashire in order to evolve methods for utilising the shorter staple cotton, which Lancashire was formerly unable to use and which will probably always remain a very large part of the Indian crop. The admirable propaganda and active work carried out by the Lancashire Indian Cotton Committee has resulted in a very striking increase in the United Kingdom's takings of Indian cotton during recent years. From 230,000 bales in 1932–33, they rose to 639,000 bales in 1936–37, and the possibilities are very far from being exhausted. The Committee said in 1935— and it is even truer in 1937 than it was then—

" It is beyond question that the educational propaganda of the last two years has had a very powerful effect in Lancashire. A definite goodwill towards Indian cotton has been brought into existence throughout the industry, and it is in sharp contrast to the attitude of mind towards Indian growths which has always obtained previously. A great many mills have made adjustments in their processes and even in equipment so as to enable them to use Indian types to advantage. A large number of new market connections have been opened, and Indian cotton has been brought into the foreground of the commercial arena in a way which has exceeded the most optimistic expectations of the Committee. All this is of comparatively recent growth and its practical effect should be more far-reaching as time goes on ".

The value of the work of the Committee ought—as I hope it is—to be specially apparent in India at the present moment when the conflict in the Far East has, as I gather from recent reports in the Press, resulted in exports of Indian cotton to Japan falling to a lower level than any reached for many years past.

My next two instances of co-operation are neither so relevant nor so satisfactory. They are not so relevant because the co-operation here is not exclusively within the Empire but is international. And they are not so satisfactory because a Conference, one of whose objects is to stress increased efficiency of production in its broadest sense, is here confronted with problems arising out of the consequences of stimulation of that production to a pitch at which consumption is definitely below it. The moral to be drawn—on which it is not necessary for me to enlarge—is the necessity for stimulating consumption not only throughout the Empire but throughout the World. The two commodities to which I refer are rubber and tea.

India, including Burma, is a party to restriction schemes in regard to both. From the Indian point of view, it is, however, satisfactory to find that, in spite of restriction, the export trade in rubber is becoming of increasing importance. The total quantity of rubber exported rose from 16.2 million pounds valued at £234,000 in 1933–34 to 30.6 million pounds valued at £665,250 in 1935–36. The corresponding figures for exports to the United Kingdom were 3.3 million pounds valued at £57,000 and 10.8 million pounds valued at £238,950. The working of the tea restriction scheme has been different. Exports have been reduced from 379 million pounds in 1932–33, the peak year, to 302 million pounds last year, but it should be mentioned that the value of the 269 million pounds imported into the United Kingdom, far the most important of India's customers for tea, in 1935 was £1½ millions more than that of the 312 million pounds imported in 1932, so that on balance the producer has gained by restriction. And the vigorous propaganda carried on in various parts of Empire by the International Tea Market Expansion Board has undoubtedly been successful in stimulating consumption. The balance retained for consumption in India in 1935–36 was estimated at 83 million pounds against 63 million pounds in 1932–33.

Jute, second only in importance to cotton in the export trade of India, is another crop which furnishes an example of the two-fold problem of restriction of production and stimulation of consumption. Since 1935, the Government of Bengal have made strenuous efforts to secure the voluntary restriction of the area under jute. Those efforts have met with some degree of success, and, in 1935, the official estimate of out-turn was 7.2 million bales against 8.5 million bales in 1934. It had increased to 8.7 million bales in 1936, but that was some two million bales less than the average for the three years 1927–29. Prices reacted to restriction, and the price of raw jute in 1935, on the whole, showed a marked appreciation over that for 1934. On the 1st October last, it was some Rs. 6 per bale higher than on October 1st of the two previous years and Rs. 8½ above that on October 1st, 1934, but how far that is due to restriction and how far to world factors, it would be rash to say. But it is all to the good that the Indian Jute Industry has at length wakened up to the dangers resulting from economic nationalism, the pro-

gress made by competing fibres such as sisal and coir, the
scientific attempts made to find suitable substitutes and
changes in methods of transport. With the assistance of Dr.
S. G. Barker, the industry is now engaged in active examination
of the problems of keeping its present markets unimpaired, of
recovering lost markets, if at all possible, and of establishing
new ones. Again, at long last, a recommendation of the Royal
Commission on Agriculture has borne fruit, and the Government of India have decided to establish a Central Jute Committee on the lines of the Indian Central Cotton Committee to
watch over the interests of all branches of the trade from the
field to the factory.

Lastly, in this connection, a word should be said about sugar,
although it is not an export crop. In 1929–30 nearly one million
tons valued at £12.2 millions were imported into India. These
imports, thanks to the stimulation of production in India
caused by a very high import duty, imposed originally for
revenue and maintained for protective purposes, have practically disappeared as the Finance Member knows to his cost.
The progress of the industry has been far too rapid to be
entirely healthy and has brought with it a new set of problems
which will shortly come under the purview of the Sugar Committee which it is proposed to establish on somewhat the same
lines as the Committees for Cotton and Jute. Sir John Russell
has recommended that this Committee should take over the
Sugar Research Institute at Cawnpore, established two or
three years ago by the Imperial Council of Agricultural Research.

I have commented at some length on the work which is being
done on the various crops in India, as I thought it would interest you to know something about the efforts which are being
made in India to improve production in various directions and
also to stimulate consumption. I now turn—rather late in the
day you may think—to the question which interests some of
you probably much more than those with which I have dealt—
the under-consumption in India of manufactured goods from
other parts of the Empire, more especially from this country. I
do so with great reluctance, for I am painfully aware that I am
now entering on very difficult and controversial ground, all
the more so because negotiations between His Majesty's

Government in this country and his Government in India are still in progress in regard to the continuance in some form or other of the Ottawa Agreement. I retired from the Government of India in April last and have had no part or lot in those negotiations. In the little I have to say on this aspect, I hope it will be quite clear that I am merely expressing my own personal views.

I have endeavoured to show how the real national income of India can be enlarged by increased efficiency throughout the countryside. Increased efficiency should bring in its train increased prosperity and increased demand for many things at present outside the villager's ken, better clothing if not more of it—I have often thought that the time has come for economic studies of the real needs of the Indian peasantry in regard to clothing—better housing, better sanitation, more books and newspapers, more bicycles, and the thousand and one luxuries which, as what we like to regard as progress advances, become necessities. A striking example of the way in which demand can spring up has been furnished by the spread of travel by motor-bus in India both among the urban and rural population—a demand which has caused the railway authorities in India considerable searching of heart.

In all discussions on Imperial development, one inevitably has to return time and again to the question of increased purchasing power. As to the need for that, there is general agreement. But when we come to the ways in which increased purchasing power is to be secured, then " *quot homines, tot sententiae.*" I am not an economist, and I can only state the position as it strikes me briefly and crudely. If the United Kingdom expects India to take her manufactured goods, it must contribute in increasing degree to the increase of Indian purchasing power. This applies, though not, of course, to the same extent, to the Dominions. Greater purchases of Indian raw products are only the first step in this direction. Rapid progress in industrialisation in India is a fact that has to be faced. The gospel of self-sufficiency is preached in India with as much zeal and as much misdirected enthusiasm as it is in some other countries. Its advocates overlook what I stressed earlier on, the importance of the export market to the cultivator. They overlook the equally important consideration that even if India produced all the manufactured goods she now imports, the amount of additional employment that would be created would be very small compared with the vast population of India. Take cotton manufactures, for instance—still, in spite of the tremendous fall in recent years, much the most important of India's imports. The best estimates available place the total amount of cotton piece goods available for consumption in India in 1913–14 at 5,280 million yards, of which 3,130 million yards were supplied by imports, 1,080 million yards by Indian mills and 1,070 million yards by handlooms. In 1935–36 the total available for consumption in India had increased to 6,130 million yards, of which only 970 million yards were supplied by imports, whereas the amount supplied by handlooms had increased to 1,660 million yards and that supplied by Indian mills had—as Lancashire knows only too well—gone up to 3,500 million yards. But the number of those employed in the cotton mills had only increased by about 200,000. If India were to manufacture all the cotton goods she now imports, that would only mean an addition to the number of those at present employed in the cotton mills of less than 100,000. If the imports were replaced by handloom products, as both they and mill products may well be to some extent now that half a dozen Provincial Governments are stout protagonists for the use of *Khaddar*, the number would, of course, be much larger, but, even so, it would be a drop in the ocean compared with the millions who are added to India's population every year.

There is one point about these figures on which this is perhaps the best place to comment. The average consumption of cloth per head in India in 1913–14 was 16.50 yards : in 1935–36 it was 16.57 yards. It varied, of course, in the interval, the lowest figure reached being 11.81 yards in 1921–22, in the period of very high prices after the War. The highest figure reached was 16.70 yards in 1932–33. I should not like to hazard a guess as to the extent to which it may be desirable that it should be exceeded. We have even less data about India's real needs in regard to clothing than we have about those in regard to diet. As I suggested at an earlier stage, they might well form the subject of some of those economic enquiries which are helping to supply the lacunæ in our information.

To revert to the point I was endeavouring to make. The

Indian Fiscal Commission did not attach overwhelming importance to the effect of industries in drawing any surplus population from the land. Their view was that " Even if the development of industries in the near future is very rapid, the population withdrawn from the land will be but a small proportion." But that is no argument against industrialisation, and there are very strong arguments in its favour—always provided that it can be accomplished without the evils which some industrial centres in India have only too faithfully copied from their Western prototypes. As I see them—I may perhaps be forgiven for repeating what I said in India in 1936—

" Those arguments are that the diversification consequent on an advance of industrialisation will render the economic life of the country less precarious than if it depends on agriculture alone, that the capital of the country will be made more mobile by opportunities of industrial investment, that a higher standard of living in the industrial centres will exert some influence in gradually raising the standard of life in the countryside, and, lastly, that industrial enterprise will have the effect of quickening initiative and practical intelligence and thereby of contributing certain new and valuable elements to the national character."

Argument or no argument, industrialisation in India is proceeding apace and must be recognised as inevitable. The last report of the India Stores Department, the Government of India's purchasing agency, gives a lengthy list of articles to which attention was specially devoted during the year in order to develop their manufacture in India and their utilisation in preference to imported articles. Gone are the days, if indeed they ever existed, when it was possible for this country or any other to dictate to India what form her industrialisation should take. That being so, it follows, I think, that the second step to be taken by this country to improve the purchasing power of India so that that country may take more of her highly-specialised manufactured goods is to purchase certain classes of Indian manufactured goods of a less specialised character and to maintain the large free market in this country for those goods. I cannot but think that, unless one takes a very short view, that that is a step which it is in the widest interests of British manufacturers and consumers generally to take. There are certain manufactures for which India has special advantages, certain classes of cotton goods, jute goods, carpets, leather, both finished and unfinished, to mention only a few of the more important. Unpleasant as it may be, it would be very unwise to fail to recognise that the centre of gravity of the world's textile industry is moving steadily East, and though this fact may call for more replanning in the British textile industries, it offers some countervailing advantages to manufacturers of machinery, chemical manufacturers and a large number of other highly specialised industries.

Time does not permit me to do more than make a passing reference to the dangers of the excessive development of bilateral trade agreements from the point of view of a country such as India, whose position as a negotiating country is weakened by the fact that at present she lives mainly by the export of raw materials and foodstuffs, and normally has to export more than she imports. They were discussed at great length last year in the Indian Legislative Assembly, and I will not repeat the arguments made by speakers on the Government benches against those members of the Opposition who held that India should scrap all her existing trade treaties and start with a clean slate. But I should like to remind you of the wording of the original resolution passed by the Ottawa Conference which ran as follows :

" The nations of the British Commonwealth having entered into certain agreements with one another for the extension of Imperial trade by means of reciprocal preferential tariffs, this Conference takes note of those Agreements and records its conviction :

That by the lowering or removal of barriers among themselves provided for in those agreements, the flow of trade between the various countries of the Empire will be facilitated, and that by the consequent increase of purchasing power of their peoples, the trade of the world will also be stimulated and increased.

Further, that this Conference regards the conclusion of these agreements as a step forward which should, in the future, tend to further progress in the same direction and which will utilise protective duties to ensure that the resources and industries of the Empire are developed on sound economic lines."

It follows, therefore, that it was the avowed aim of the Government of the United Kingdom so to develop its policy of Imperial Preference that it would lead to freer trade within the Empire and thus eventually to freer trade within the world in general. That policy in so far—and this is an important qualification—as it was consistent with the protection of British industries has been pursued since Ottawa. This has been possible for the United Kingdom because it was so long a Free Trade country and is still, in essence, a country of low tariffs in which direct taxation is high and indirect taxation, except for a few special articles of great importance, such as tea and tobacco, comparatively low, so that customs revenue is relatively unimportant.

The problem, as we know to our cost, is very different in India. If bilateral agreements are to assist the development of world trade as well as of Empire trade, it seems to follow that tariff preferences should not be sought on imports which are extremely important to non-Empire countries and discrimination against which might lead to trade dislocation and the raising or consolidation of barriers against trade. Trade agreements and tariff preferences by themselves do not ensure increased consumption, and, whilst Empire sentiment cannot and should not be ignored, even more importance should, I think, be extended to serious studies of the needs of consuming countries and the abilities of producing countries. It is, I am sure, unnecessary to develop this point further for an audience such as this. I would only refer once again, as an example of what I have in mind, to the work of the Indian Central Cotton Committee in co-operation with the Lancashire Indian Cotton Committee and, more recently, of the Indian Coffee-Marketing Expansion Board in London, a branch of the Indian Coffee Cess Committee in India.

It is, I think, of great significance that our discussions here should be almost coincident with the appointment of an eminent economist, Professor Gregory, to assist the Government of India in working out the problems which are engaging the attention of this Conference.

Let me end as I began with apologising for my imperfections. Few speakers can ever have been given wider terms of reference than those which have been given to the speakers at this Conference. My subject has been so vast that I have only been able to dwell on a few points and have been compelled to omit many of very great importance. I ought, I know, to have said something about the possibilities of further large irrigation works in India, about the Marketing Surveys which it is hoped will lead to marked improvements in the conditions in which some of India's major crops are marketed, about the co-operative movement, once so full of promise, but the fire of which has died down, though the embers are still capable of being fanned into a flame at which the Indian peasantry can warm its hands, if not its whole body—and about many other subjects. But my time and your patience are alike limited, and I can only hope that the *disjecta membra* I have put before you, establishing, as I trust they have, that India's contribution to an increase in Empire prosperity can only be secured by concerted, strenuous and sustained effort to raise the standard of living in the Indian village will elicit a lively discussion amongst those more competent to speak than I am.

The discussion was opened by :

Sir JOHN MAYNARD[1]: The address of Sir Frank Noyce has opened up rivers of discussion. I am only capable of dealing with two very small rills that issue from those rivers.

In the first place I want to stress this point, that one of the things from which India is suffering is under-employment in the villages. For that reason there was one point on which I felt inclined to differ from what Sir Frank Noyce said. I understood him to say that we should try to keep the people on the land. I submit that that is not a policy which is reconcilable with the fact that there are enormous numbers in the villages who have not sufficient work to do. It is because they are unable to do more than they actually do at the present that the country is economically a poor one. It is necessary to deal with this evil of under-employment in the villages. For that

---

[1] MAYNARD, Sir John, K.C.I.E., late I.C.S. Member of the Executive Council of the Governor of the Punjab, 1921–26. Financial Commissioner, Punjab, 1913–20.

purpose it is clearly necessary to adopt a policy of very vigorous industrialisation, and in doing that, to think more of the good of India herself than of the good of her partners in the Empire. Both must be considered, but the first selection is the economic good of India herself. There must somehow be an end to this under-employment in the villages, and that is clearly to be reached by industrialisation and preferably by the creation of small local industrial centres with an agricultural clientéle providing them with the necessary raw materials as well as with the varieties of food which a small town population is likely to demand. This will assist agriculture indirectly by the stimulus it will give to a greater variety of production.

The second point I wish to make is that at present the quality of research in India is of a very high order indeed. It is probable that the results of that research are not made fully available because it is not brought home sufficiently to the business and bosoms of men, that is to say, the discoveries which have been made by our agricultural research are not at present being made use of, and it is necessary to find some method by which they may be more fully applied. On that point I may say something which I know is extremely heterodox, but it must be said, even if only to be demolished by succeeding speakers.

It appears to me that it is absolutely necessary, in order to bring science to bear on agriculture and in order to make a more economic use of machinery in agriculture, that attempts should be made to substitute large-scale cultivation for small-scale cultivation in India. There are two ways in which it can be done, in part by inducing great landlords, in those districts where they exist, to abandon their present attitude, which I fear is for the most part one of mere rent-receivers, and to take a vigorous and personal interest in the agriculture from which they draw their revenue. Some of our great landowners in this country have home farms of their own, and landowners in India must have them also.

That is one of the ways in which large-scale cultivation may be made possible. Another way is the development of co-opera-tive tillage. This means more than co-operative purchase and sale ; it means the co-operation in tillage of persons who will hire their agricultural machinery from depots established for that purpose, as they should be under the system I have in view. A great effort should be made to introduce co-operative tillage with large-scale cultivation.

I realise that many will be inclined to say that if we adopt a plan of this kind we are imitating a certain great country in the East of Europe whose economic ideals do not tally with those of a capitalist country, but these are my concluding words—I submit that the best way to deal with the danger of communism is to show that individualism can do equally well.

Sir ALAN GREEN[1]: I wish to thank the Chairman for his welcome : it was a great privilege to serve India at India House, as well as in India. When I was asked if I would like to listen to Sir Frank Noyce I said, " Yes," and was quickly told that I must pay for the privilege by making a speech myself. Consequently, I devoted some of my week-end leisure to extracting and studying statistics relating to India's staple products. But as anybody who knows Sir Frank and his work in India should have realised, I find myself forestalled by the contents of a very comprehensive paper. I will therefore discard my statistics and try and base my remarks on more general considerations.

I agree with nearly everything that Sir Frank Noyce has said. I am not sure, however, that I do not perceive one slight, though rather important, inconsistency. Sir Frank very reasonably wants to see the standard of living in India raised. He also wants to see the Empire, and the world, buying more extensively from India, in order to render possible that improved standard of living. On the other hand, I will not say that he looks with disfavour on cash crops : he admits they are necessary, but he does point out that food crops should be improved —that they should be to a certain extent altered in their nature, and that they should be consumed in larger quantities in India. If India is to consume more of her food-stuffs and is to restrict the cultivation of cash crops, I fear that she will not receive that income from the export market which is so essential for her, if she is to maintain and still more if she is to improve her standard of living.

[1] GREEN, Sir Alan Michael, C.I.E., late I.C.S. Under-Secretary, Government of India, Commerce and Industries Department, 1918. Deputy High Commissioner for India in the United Kingdom, 1930–4. Assistant Secretary of the Imperial Economic Committee.

I am not sure, however, that there is any real antagonism. I always marvel when I think of India, not only at the immensity of the country and her population, but also at the immensity of her production. I said I would discard statistics, but if I may give a few round figures, it is worth recalling that India produces each year something like three and a half million hundredweight of tea, a million tons of cotton, two million tons of jute, three million tons of ground nuts, ten million tons of wheat, and thirty to thirty-five million tons of rice. Those figures of course include Burma, for I agree with Sir Frank that the time has not yet come to separate, statistically, India from Burma.

In the export field, from that great production India does sell overseas very considerable quantities. She could not have the balance of trade she enjoys if she did not. And yet if the figures are examined, it will be found that in many instances it is only a relatively small proportion of the total output that is exported, only the surplus not required for home consumption. Of course there are crops which are mostly or largely exported, such as tea, cotton, jute and some oil seeds, but the position is not to-day entirely what it was even within my own memory. Take for example, wheat. Not many years ago, before the War, India was frequently one of the important world exporters. Only a short time before the War, Karachi exported in one year more wheat than any other port in the world. But India is eating much more wheat now than she used to do, which is not surprising if only in view of the increase in her population. The export of wheat has dwindled down until now it is almost insignificant. I am not suggesting that India should produce much more wheat and thrust it on to a world market, which has been recently glutted, and which may possibly be glutted again before long, but wheat does perhaps point a warning that if India is to maintain her favourable balance of trade, she must export, and export largely, and that if she loses one export trade she must find another to replace it.

If India is to sell more, I submit that she must do all she can to help her customers to buy. She must not rely on selling surpluses only when she has them and finds it convenient to sell. She might perhaps do more to cultivate export markets by concentrating on greater regularity of supply. She might satisfy good customers in a year of scarcity even at the expense of her own home consumers. That may sound drastic, but it is a policy adopted with success by several exporting countries. But there are other ways of maintaining exports and persuading customers to buy from her.

I was glad to hear Sir Frank refer to the Agricultural Marketing Adviser's department. This was only started a few years ago, and from my own experience, I know it is progressing much faster than even an optimist would have thought possible. To give one example, which may seem odd, I cite tobacco. India produces nearly one-quarter of all the tobacco produced in the world, but she exports only 2 per cent of that production. That leaves her as but a small exporter by world standards. Only a few years ago she had no tobacco that could be called good, but in the last few years she has paid so much attention to quality, type and curing that she now produces tobacco that is definitely good. Now, owing to the marketing adviser's initiative, she has grading and marking regulations. If you are interested enough to read the Report of the Imperial Economic Committee on Tobacco, you will see that there are certainly great possibilities about the export of improved tobacco, and of a very valuable and extended trade for India in that commodity.

I would then make these two points, that India must help her clients to buy from her by guaranteeing, within reason, regularity of supply, and that she must constantly strive to improve quality and grading. Then she may hope to increase the value of her exports, and win a cash return that will do something towards improving her standard of life.

Sir SELWYN FREMANTLE[1]: I think we have all enjoyed and appreciated to the full that description, complete so far as is possible, of the economic life of India which Sir Frank Noyce has given us, and no one is better qualified to give such an address. I am not going to be the one to quarrel with his recommendations of how—what I believe to be the object of this Conference—the increase of production and increase of consumption can be brought about so far as India is concerned.

[1] FREMANTLE, Sir Selwyn Howe, C.S.I., C.I.E., late I.C.S. Member of Council of the Lieut.-Governor of the United Provinces, India, 1920. Member of the Board of Revenue of the United Provinces, 1921. Served on the Committee on Emigration from India to the Crown Colonies.

I would like, as I cannot contend with the lecturer, to contend with the first speaker after him, Sir John Maynard, when he referred to unemployment of the villages and seemed to think that that could be remedied by industrialisation. Sir Frank Noyce has given us some interesting figures of the sinister increase of population in India. He said that in the last decennial period there had been an enormous increase of 38 million people.

Not long ago an address on population was given to the East Indian Association by Professor Radha Kamal Miekheyi of Lucknow, and in that he compared this figure of 38 millions with the figure of the number of people supported by industries in India, which came to 35 million. Therefore the increase in ten years in India's population is greater than the total number of people supported by industry in the country. Does not that show how very small a proportion of the increase of population can be absorbed in industry ?

It seems obvious then, from these population figures, that when you speak of the improvement of the standard of living of the Indian masses, you must refer almost entirely to the agricultural masses, and this improvement is not entirely an economic problem. The Agricultural Commission laid stress on the fact that mere material improvement alone will not bring lasting benefit to the people, for it will merely postpone the effects of the great pressure of population on the land. It is the desire for a higher standard of living that will furnish the demand. That gives the essence of the problem. We know that many organisations, missions, Y.M.C.A.'s and Indian organisations alike have been attacking the problem of rural inertia in a small and sporadic way. They have not been able from their lack of resources to make much impression on the country as a whole. The Government has only recently taken up the problem in earnest. The fact that rural reconstruction has been so long delayed is due primarily to the absorption of the Indian intelligentsia in political matters.

Within the last few years matters have changed. There have been Rural Development Commissioners appointed in various Provinces together with Departments for rural reconstruction and improvement, and in all the provinces of Northern India a great deal has been done. The idea generally is to start a campaign from all sides at once on this rural inertia, to make use of all the Government Departments and experts in bringing about an improvement of life in the villages. But it is an expensive business, and it cannot be too much diffused or it will have no effect. I think that that process, which is absolutely necessary, would be greatly expedited if the necessity for organising the village were better recognised. However that may be, the foundations of the development of rural reconstruction have been laid, and all that we can do here at the present time seems to be to encourage the efforts being made in that direction. They must inevitably in time bring about a rise in the standard of living and it is by that that India will make her contribution to an increase in the Empire's trade.

Sir HENRY LAWRENCE[1]: It is ten years and more since I left India, so it is with some anxiety and modesty that I venture to add one or two words to what Sir Frank Noyce has put before us. I suppose it was rather a shock to many to realise that the gravest problem that is going to fall to the lot of the Indian Governments now coming into power to deal with is the problem of feeding the enormous increase of population that is pouring forth in that country year by year. The last census recorded an increase of thirty millions. It is clearly beyond the competence of a Government to control natural fertility : and its relation to the precepts of certain religions which enjoin fertility has placed the subject outside the sphere of action of a British administration.

Some Indian friends of mine were discussing the subject recently, and one observed, " I have seven sons but I do not consider that my duty to the country is yet fully discharged." Mr. Gandhi in one of the phases of his policy of Non-Co-operation with the British Government urged his followers to breed no more children, but the efficacy of his advice seems to be discounted by that portentous increase of thirty millions. How are these new millions to be fed ?

Two roads suggest themselves : Emigration and Industrialisation.

[1] LAWRENCE, Sir Henry, K.C.S.I., late I.C.S. Secretary to the Government of Bombay, Director of Agriculture. Commissioner in Sind, 1916–20. Member of the Council of the Governor of Bombay, 1921–26. Member of the Royal Commission on Agriculture in India, 1926–28.

F

Some colonies of Indians are to be found in every part of the world ; some of the most hardy and successful emigrated from the province I knew best—Sind on the North-West frontier. They were merchants trading in Central Asia and in every sea-port in the Seven Seas. Thirty years ago other Sindis established a Camel Transport business in Northern Australia.

During the War I spoke to wounded Indian soldiers from Mesopotamia, who expressed their desire to go back and settle there if lands could be given to them. Vacant lands there are in plenty in Australia, Africa, Arabia and Mesopotamia, if the present inhabitants could be persuaded to welcome immigrants.

Take the wars on the North-West Frontier. These are due to the economic pressure on tribes who cannot earn a living in those barren highlands. So also on the Eastern Frontier. I was present when the chiefs of head-hunting tribes there asked the Chairman of a Royal Commission for permission to pursue their head-hunting forays, first because it was the only occupation worthy of a man, and second because it was the best method known to them of the economic appeasement of their region.

It would be well worth while for the State to enquire what assistance in emigration can be given to such men pining for an outlet for their energies.

In regard to industrialisation, over 70 per cent of the population live by agriculture ; and industrial occupations increase very slowly. British administrators who in the last generation were brought up to believe that Free Trade was the right policy for Great Britain and for the world, could not be persuaded of the justice and wisdom of affording Protection to the infant industries of India. As the influence in the Government of Indian politicians increased, tentative efforts at protection were made, but with marked hesitation. Meantime the universities have been turning out large numbers of young men educated in the sciences, and the pressure of their unemployment has generated much discontent and recruited the ranks of disaffected black-coated youth.

There is bound to be a conflict between the agricultural and the industrial interests, and national pride is likely to be enlisted on the side of a self-contained India. We have seen how determined the statesmen of the Dominions have been to establish their own industries ; and we may be sure that the statesmen of India will study their policies.

I hesitate to speak of individual industries, and will only refer to two with which I came in contact when I handled the finances of the Bombay Presidency.

The Tata group of Iron and Steel, and Hydro-Electric works was founded in the face of severe discouragement from English financiers and pseudo-scientific geologists. This is a gigantic concern and India may well be proud of its financial and industrial management. The latest arrival is sugar. For many years I have pointed out that the protection of sugar is necessary firstly in the interests of the three millions of families who live by it, and secondly for the employment of Indians educated in the sciences. No industry covers a wider field of science : men are required for irrigation—soil preparation, selection of seed, prevention of pests, scientific cultivation, all branches of agriculture—and then follow the countless processes of the manufacture of refined sugar in the factories, and the subsequent marketing. But sugar has no friends at Court, and the infant Hercules is in danger of being sacrificed on the altar of Free Trade.

It is probable, however, that India will enter on a course of high tariffs, and that the last vestiges of the Free Trade system of the last generation will disappear.

When we consider the immensity of the scale on which these changes have been carried out in India—changes which affect the mode of life and government of 350 millions of people, we may pay a tribute to the orderly character of the people and to the wisdom and restraint of the classes who have been placed in a new position of power. We may also appreciate the burden of responsibility which falls on the shoulders of the Viceroy and of his chief councillors, amongst whom Sir Frank Noyce and our Chairman have held a high place.

Sir JOSEPH SMITH[1]: The previous speaker has referred to the alarm with which he listened to Sir Frank Noyce stressing, if not deliberately advocating, the shrinkage of cash crops in order to stimulate the agricultural food crops. I do not know if I

---

[1] SMITH, Sir Joseph, C.I.E. Secretary to the Government of the Punjab Irrigation Department (retd.). Member of the Central Board of Irrigation, India, 1931–32.

understood Sir Frank aright, but if he is going to raise the standard of living of the country, there must be an exportable surplus from the cash crops. I am not particularly distressed about that. Other speakers have handled it, and I have no doubt that in its proper place it will get adequate attention. What I was really disturbed to observe was that the time was not far distant when the food crops will fall short of the requirements of the people of the country. That is a very serious situation that is likely to arise. A previous speaker has mentioned how within his knowledge wheat exports from India fell very considerably from what they once were, until to-day they are practically negligible.

Another point that Sir Frank mentioned was that sufficient agricultural land is not available for the extension of cultivation. I speak with knowledge of the Punjab only, and it is possible that the conditions in the Punjab do not obtain in other parts of India. I am not competent to speak for the rest of India, so confine myself to the Punjab only, where there are many thousands of acres where agriculture with irrigation could produce, at any rate, a certain proportion of what is likely to be required by that growing population.

Sir John Maynard stressed the desirability of linking industry with agriculture. Personally I am a great believer in that. I cannot refrain from quoting what that great man of industry, Henry Ford, has said, that " with one leg on the land and the other in industry, almost any country can be self-sufficing ". It is not my point to recommend that India should be self-sufficing, but the stimulating of industry and the coupling of it to agriculture, can do a great deal.

Sir John also referred to co-operative tillage. There again do I see great possibilities. I am not an economist, but just a straightforward engineer who spent thirty years in the irrigation service of the Punjab. History does not repeat itself, but it repeats its lesson. So I would conclude with one observation from my own experience. When I first went to the Punjab conditions were such that to get anything like a specialised bolt we had to send to Bombay or Calcutta, two thousand miles away. Before I left, owing to the expansion following on irrigation and extension of agriculture, not only could we get a bolt but all kinds of delicate implements, in fact, everything required could be obtained, if not in Lahore, within a very short while of the order being placed there. That is what followed in the footsteps of an expanding agriculture.

Sir FIROZKHAN NOON : I think it is your wish that I should thank Sir Frank Noyce for his excellent paper. He has given us some very illuminating figures and facts, and I should like to draw your attention to one or two things in his address which stand out distinctly from an Empire point of view. He has pointed out to you what a low standard of living prevails in the whole of India, and when you compare that with the high standard of living in New Zealand, Australia, South Africa, Canada and England, it is then that the possible repercussions of that situation on the economic relations of the various parts of this great Empire will be realised. India is already one of the eight leading industrial countries of the world, and I am sure that within the next twenty or thirty years, given the necessary capital expenditure, India will industrialise still further and expand her interests in the world markets for industrial products. From some of the indications which have been given by Sir Frank Noyce, it will be realised that India's competitive position in world trade and industry is strong, and with improvement in efficiency it will rapidly become much stronger. This is particularly so with those Indian industries whose raw materials are produced in India, outstanding examples of which are the jute mill and the cotton mill industries. With the raw materials at her door and cheap labour in abundance, it is only natural to expect that India's manufactured products will be marketed at highly competitive prices.

We may take the case of cotton to-day. India is producing about 80 per cent of the mill-made cloth consumed in India. It has been shown that her consumption of cloth per head is very much the same to-day as it was in 1914. With India's poverty and her low standard of living, the Lancashire manufacturer with his high cost of production has not much prospect of finding consumers for his expensive cloth unless the purchasing power of the farmer in India is increased. Nor can he expect to compete with Indian mills in producing the cheap cloth which will continue to be consumed in India so long as the standard of life remains at its present low level.

The time has arrived when all friends of India should attempt to raise the standard of living in India so that it may approach more closely to the standard of living in other parts of the Empire. This is a matter of importance to the rest of the Empire as well as to India ; and I do not agree with those who hold the view that it is impossible to raise the standard of living of a nation by external influences. There are nations in the world who have shown how the standard of living can be raised, and in India it will be raised only by one means, namely, by raising the income of the agriculturist. I know that in the short run the interests of the agricultural producer and the manufacturer both in India and abroad do not always run parallel. The manufacturer of cloth in Lancashire and India naturally wants cheap cotton, while the producer of cotton always looks with pleasure on an increasing price for his product ; but unless the return to the agriculturist in India is greatly increased, there is no hope of India consuming, in increasing quantity, the expensive goods manufactured in other parts of the world.

These economic problems are of the highest importance to India and to the Empire as a whole, and it is for this reason that I welcome the step recently taken by the Government of India in appointing Professor Gregory as their Economic Adviser. India to-day needs the advice of all the economists she can employ, so that the Government of India may be able to plan their economic policy with a view to raising the standard of living in India and the purchasing power of her people. Unless this is done, I am afraid this co-operation and friendliness within the Empire will be mere talk, leading nowhere, while the standard of living in India and in other parts of the Empire will remain poles apart and continue to be a constant source of friction among the various parts of the Empire. To me the agricultural drive of the Government of India is particularly welcome, because the welfare of the village farmer means the welfare of India.

I think that, from the Empire point of view, the lecturer has done a great service in pointing out that unless the purchasing power of India is raised there cannot be industrial and economic peace with India.

REPLY

Sir FRANK NOYCE : I have to thank you for your all too generous reference to my work in India. I have to thank my audience for their very cordial reception of a speech which I feel was too highly spiced with a number of statistics, and the speakers who either brought out new points, like Sir Henry Lawrence, on the possibility of future migration in the Empire, or who have enlarged points with which time did not enable me to deal fully.

There are only two points on which I should like to comment. One was the inconsistency referred to by Sir Alan Green. Sir Joseph Smith also felt the same difficulty, that I was a little inconsistent in arguing that cash crops in India should be reduced, and at the same time asking the United Kingdom and other parts of the Empire to take more of India's raw materials. I do not think there is any real inconsistency. I think there is room for both; if not, why is it necessary to restrict crops like jute, tea, rubber and the like ? The real answer to the point is that India wants more scientific planning of crops all round.

Sir John Maynard referred to the drift to the towns. The point he raised shows how difficult it is in a paper covering so large a field to explain oneself as fully as one would like. Sir John was anxious to see something more than a drift to the towns—a rapid rush. Sir Selwyn Fremantle dealt adequately with this point. Rapid industrialisation is not a panacea for all India's economic ills, but would lead to a better balance of her economic life. If there is a drift to the towns, one hopes that it will not be to the great centres like Bombay, Allahabad and Calcutta, but to new centres in healthy surroundings.

What I had in mind was the desirability of keeping on the land the educated classes who can make the village a much happier place than it is at present. I was not thinking of the agricultural labourer who is not employed for the great part of the year, but I referred to the young men who wanted Government jobs and who could find such useful niches in the countryside if Indian country life were anything like what it ought to be, or used to be in the West. Those are the people we want to keep on the land, people who can make a real contribution to raising the standard of village life, which I am glad to find everyone agrees is so vital to the increased prosperity of India and of the Empire.

III

THE COLONIES AND THE PROBLEM

Wednesday, November 24th. Morning Session

Sir JOHN CHANCELLOR[1]: It is my privilege to introduce to you Lord Dufferin, Under-Secretary of State for the Colonies, who will address you on the subject of the Colonies—truly a wide subject—and one of supreme importance to-day both imperially and internationally.

It is interesting to consider the various phases through which public opinion has passed in regard to the relationship of the Mother Country to the Colonies. These phases have changed in accordance with the changes in the spirit of the times through which we have lived.

In the eighteenth century the Colonies were regarded as the absolute property of the United Kingdom ; and it was thought right that their resources should be exploited and their trade controlled primarily in the interest of the Mother Country.

In the nineteenth century the doctrines of free trade and *laisser-faire* obtained such ascendancy in the public mind that no one could speak against them or even point out that the purely economic considerations which inspired them did not embrace every aspect of our relations with the Colonies. It was then that that hypothetical figure of the Victorian Age—the economic man, animated by motives of self-interest, more or less enlightened—appeared on the scene and became an important factor in guiding our policy.

As the result of those theories, views as to our relations with the Colonies changed, and it was thought that our duties to

---

[1] CHANCELLOR, Sir John, G.C.M.G., G.C.V.O., D.S O , late R.E. Assistant Secretary to Committee of Imperial Defence, 1904. Secretary to the Colonial Defence Committee, 1906. Governor of Mauritius, 1911–16 ; of Trinidad and Tobago, 1916–21. Governor of Southern Rhodesia, 1923–28 ; High Commissioner and Commander-in-Chief, Palestine, 1928–31. Chairman of the Agricultural Marketing Facilities Committee, of the Permanent Joint Hops Committee and of the Cattle Committee.

them were fully discharged, when we guaranteed their security from external aggression and granted them freedom of trade.

Nothing was done to promote the internal trade of the Empire. The Colonies enjoyed no preference for their produce in the markets of the United Kingdom. They were left to take their chance in competition with other countries in the world's markets. There was even a certain school of thought that wanted to get rid of the Colonies altogether.

When I went to Mauritius as Governor twenty-six years ago, of the sugar crop amounting to about one-quarter of a million tons, practically none used to be imported into the United Kingdom. Our nearest markets geographically—Australia and South Africa—were practically closed to Mauritius sugar by high import duties. Mauritius sugar found its chief markets in India and on the continent of Europe.

I well remember that when we used to pray for rain when drought threatened the crop, we used also to offer up un-Christian prayers that misfortunes might befall the countries which were our competitors in the sugar markets of the world, and so bring about a rise in the price of sugar. We used to pray for a drought in Europe, for a revolution in Cuba and for something else—a rising of the Acheen I think it was—in Java. Our impious prayers were not always answered; and the consequences were the periodical vicissitudes in the fortunes of our sugar Colonies of which you are aware.

It was not until the War came and brought many changes of outlook that the possibility of obtaining for Colonial sugar a preference in the British market entered the region of practical politics. At first preference was granted for a year only, being voted in the Budget each year.

I was in Trinidad at that time, and my planter friends urged me to press His Majesty's Government to guarantee a preference for a period of ten years in order to enable them to put capital into the industry—to develop their estates and to purchase new machinery—with a reasonable prospect of obtaining a return for their expenditure. I told them (that was in 1916, when opinion in party politics in the United Kingdom was sharply divided and when protection was still a long way off) that there was no hope of a British Government so committing itself and its successors. It was not until after the War when a catastrophic fall in the price of sugar from over £100 to £4—£5 per ton, bringing ruin to the planters and disaster to the sugar Colonies, that Colonial preference became a generally accepted part of our fiscal system.

One direct consequence of that preference, I am glad to know, is that since I left Trinidad its sugar crop has increased by over 100 per cent, and to-day almost the whole of the Mauritius crop now comes to the United Kingdom.

The terrible experiences of the War have led to another change in our relations with the Colonies.

It is now recognised by all schools of thought in this country that our relations to our Colonies are those of a guardian or trustee to his wards : that we must safeguard their interests, that we must develop their trade and their resources in the interest of their populations and not in the interests of the people of the United Kingdom.

The recognition of that relationship of trustee to ward has been happily demonstrated by His Majesty's Government by the creation in 1929 of the Colonial Development Advisory Committee, which provides money on loan and by grant for the development of the resources of the Colonies. And it is only a few weeks ago that the Secretary of State for the Colonies announced the establishment of the Colonial Empire Marketing Board to do for the Colonies what the Empire Marketing Board was to do for the Dominions. I wish it all success in its activities.

I have now great pleasure in inviting Lord Dufferin to address you. As Under-Secretary of State for the Colonies, he is too well known to you all to require any detailed commendation from me.

THE MARQUESS OF DUFFERIN AND AVA[1]: I need hardly tell you how deeply I appreciate the honour which has fallen to me by being asked to address you in this building in which I have been preceded by so many eminent speakers. I would like at once to express my full consciousness that that honour has fallen to me more out of respect to the office that I hold than to the personality that holds it. I would only say in passing, that I hope the fruits of this Conference will not be less than those

[1] DUFFERIN AND AVA, Basil Sheridan Hamilton-Temple-Blackwood, 4th MARQUESS of. Parliamentary Under-Secretary of State for the Colonies.

of the other Conferences which have been held under the
auspices of this distinguished Society.

As I understand, it is the object of the present Conference to
discuss various aspects of the problem of Empire development,
and it falls to me to open the discussion of development of the
Colonial Empire. It will be my task to show you that that problem is not merely different from all other problems of Empire
development ; it is not one problem, but many. It will not
be possible for me to express to you the problem in terms of
x and y, and to say " There is the problem : here are three
hundred and forty-five ways of meeting it, and for various
reasons we have chosen this one " : on the contrary, I hope to
show that it is not a single problem but a whole host of problems.

Before I begin on that, I would say a word about some of the
other indications of the word ' development '. Our task presumably in the Colonial Office is to lead Colonial people to a
larger and a fuller life, to make them capable of realising their
own potentialities and to enable them to appreciate the moral
standards and ethical values upon which we in Europe set
store. That implies quite clearly many other things besides
merely material prosperity. It means the development of
social and political institutions : it means the steady increase of
educational facilities : it means the improvement of the health
of the communities and, above all, it means the inculcation by
precept and by example of certain ethical and moral standards
to which we attach importance. In fact, one of the main difficulties of the Colonial Department seems to be to keep this
ethical and moral development in step with the material development which we pursue at the same time. Of course that is no
new problem either to the Colonial Empire or to the world as a
whole. The main reason why the history of mankind can best
be understood as the history of a lunatic, is that the intellectual
achievements of mankind have seldom kept step with moral
developments. Either one lobe or the other of the lunatic's
brain is always in advance, and at this moment we see in
Europe the lunatic's hand, more and more cunning at devising
the material instruments of destruction, while his moral forces
seem incapable of restraining him. So it is in a lesser and simpler
degree with our Colonial Empire. The sudden access of wealth

to poor communities does not in itself bring happiness any more than the sudden access of drink to a teetotaller necessarily brings him happiness. We by trial and error have discovered certain moral principles by which the use of wealth may properly be governed, and it is our plain duty to bring those principles before the people to whom we are giving this new wealth that material development implies.

I say that because I do not wish you to think that if I concentrate here mainly on material resources, it is not because I overlook the other forms of development, or underrate their importance, but I imagine that the main object of this Conference is more to deal with the material side of the development of the Colonial Empire, and it is to that that I wish to address my main remarks.

What are the main objects and methods of our Colonial development on the material side ? I cannot do better than to quote from the opening speech of my Secretary of State, Mr. Ormsby Gore at the first meeting of the Colonial Empire Marketing Board in October, 1937. He wished to explain to the Board what he thought their functions would be, but he thought that it was necessary first to say something of general British Colonial policy. He said :

" We are not a Colonial Power simply for what we in this island can get out of it. Whatever the circumstances in which we assumed control of the various territories which now make up the Colonial Empire—and these circumstances are by no means uniform—it is now the settled policy of all United Kingdom Governments to be guided in their Colonial policy by the doctrine of trusteeship for Colonial populations and their interests. We fully accept the position that it is our duty to advance to the fullest possible degree the interests of the Colonial territories under our charge. . . . Poor as the United Kingdom is in raw materials of every kind, unable as it is to feed more than a comparatively small part of its people from the produce of its soil, we never have forced and we never shall force Colonial territories to produce some particular kind of goods simply because the United Kingdom happens to be short of them, irrespective of whether the Colonies happen to be well suited to produce such goods or themselves desire to produce them. Quite apart from the fact that such a policy of compulsion would be repugnant to British sentiment, we do not even believe that it would be a satisfactory basis for a sound economic structure. Even if the result is that for many of our most essential needs we have to depend on the vicissitudes of foreign trade, our policy still is to guide Colonial territories to produce those kind of goods which it is most advantageous for them to produce economically."

That is the latest statement of many which the present Secretary of State and his predecessors have made with regard to our economic policy in the Colonial Empire, and I would draw your special attention to the fact that he referred to our policy as being one of ' guiding ' Colonial territories to produce those kinds of goods which are most advantageous for them to produce economically. We do not believe that it is sound policy, nor indeed do we think that it is even practicable to order Colonial peoples to produce some particular kind of article even for their own good. We feel that the right course is to point out to them that it is for their own good to produce some particular kind of article. We try to explain to them why it is for their own good, and when they start to produce those articles, we try to help them to produce them in the best possible way. We feel quite sure that on a long view it will be better for Colonial territories and for the Empire as a whole to follow a policy of persuasion and education like this and not a policy of compulsion, which is bound to break down sooner or later, because you cannot compel the 60 million people of the Colonial Empire to do this thing or that with the few thousands of European officials who are scattered throughout it.

We belive that with the present tendency in the world to-day, and an inevitable increase in national feeling growing all over the world, that a policy of compulsion would break down sooner or later, and with its breakdown would come the disruption of the whole Colonial Empire.

I said at the beginning of my speech that we had not a single problem but a whole host of problems. This arises from the fact that there is an enormous variation between the conditions in the various Dependencies which make up the Colonial Empire.

Climatically they vary from the tropical conditions of those Dependencies in Africa and Southern Asia which lie right on the Equator to the perpetual snow and ice of the Dependencies of the Falkland Islands with almost every variety of climate between the two. It is, however, fair to say that by far the greater part of the Colonial Empire lies in the tropics.

Racially we have almost every kind of human being that there is ; inhabitants of the British Isles and their descendants and several other kinds of Europeans ; of Asiatics we have Malays, Chinese, Indians, Turks, Arabs and many others ; Africans of almost every kind except Berbers and pygmies, and in addition Polynesians, Melanesian and American aboriginals, let alone a great variety of peoples of mixed race.

Linguistically, we have either as official languages or at any rate as languages in common use well over a hundred languages, even if unimportant dialects be excluded, belonging to nearly every family of languages in the world.

In economic matters there is perhaps rather greater uniformity. The vast majority of the inhabitants of the Colonial Empire live by primary production. There is, it is true, a certain amount of industrial production, but there are very few dependencies, for practical purposes only Hong Kong and the Straits Settlements, where manufacturing industry plays an important rôle in the economic life of the community. Entrepôt trade is of importance to a few Dependencies. It is, for example, the principal activity of the Straits Settlements, Hong Kong, Aden, Malta and Gibraltar, supplemented in the last two cases by the other activities incidental to their position as important naval and military centres. A few Dependencies, too, find an important scope for their activities in the tourist traffic : Bermuda, which indeed has little else to support it, the Bahamas and several other West Indian Colonies, Malta, Cyprus and parts of East Africa. As communications improve, the tourist traffic is likely to become more rather than less important, but there are few places where it will ever be an important part of the economic structure.

But all these other possibilities put together amount to very little in the development programme compared to primary production, and within the sphere of primary production agriculture is of paramount importance.

There is a certain amount of mineral production, of course, but it is very much localised. Tin in Malaya and Nigeria, gold produced in considerable quantities in the Gold Coast and half a dozen other Dependencies, and in small quantities in another half dozen ; copper in Northern Rhodesia and Cyprus, mineral oil in Trinidad and the Dependencies in Borneo, diamonds in the Gold Coast and Sierra Leone, iron ore in Sierra Leone and Malaya, manganese in the Gold Coast, and a few other minerals of lesser importance.

Forestry is of great importance in the internal economic life of a number of Dependencies, but is still only of minor importance in the export trade.

Fisheries are of even less importance, and in the export trade practically negligible.

Thus if we are considering the question of Colonial development, while we must not overlook the possibility of development in other directions, we must inevitably think principally of agricultural development.

Even in the agricultural sphere there is less variety of production for export than might have been expected. There is, of course, a great variety of production for internal use, and if we included all the minor exports of which some mention is made in Colonial trade returns we could make a fairly long list ; but the big staples are relatively few. If we take the consolidated returns for 1935, that is, a list of the domestic exports of the whole Colonial Empire put together, we find that in that year there were only about fifteen products, of which exports exceeded an aggregate value of over £1 million each. These are rubber, tea, sugar, cocoa, palm oil and kernels, cotton, citrus fruit, ground nuts, bananas, copra, fibres other than cotton, coffee, spices and condiments, coconut oil and hides and skins. In 1936 canned pineapples probably ought to be added to the list.

Now there is this difference between agricultural development in the Colonial Empire and that in many other parts of the Empire outside the United Kingdom, and that is that the internal market is and is likely to remain far more important than the export market in most Dependencies.

As I have said, the first object of Colonial development is to enable Colonial peoples to lead happier and fuller lives.

Better health must come very high in our list of objectives, and there can be no doubt that in attaining that objective improved nutrition is an instrument of primary importance. Now under Colonial conditions improved nutrition is dependent to an overwhelming extent on greater local production of nutritious foods. The possibility of greater importation of foods of high nutritional value into the Colonial Empire is strictly limited by considerations of cost. The vast majority of Colonial peoples live exclusively on foodstuffs produced by themselves or their immediate neighbours. The only Dependencies which import foodstuffs on a really large scale are Hong Kong, Malaya and Ceylon, all of which import rice in large quantities and also various other kinds of foodstuffs. A few of the most thickly populated and smallest Dependencies import a large proportion of their foodstuffs, but generally speaking the remainder import only luxuries with which at a pinch they could dispense. The food which is produced locally is exceedingly cheap. Wages, which by English standards would be fantastically low are, in fact, quite adequate because the local foodstuffs are so cheap, but they would not be sufficient to pay for imported foodstuffs, if only because of the heavy cost of transport.

Thus the problem of improved nutrition in the Colonial Empire is almost exclusively one of finding valuable nutritive foods which can be produced locally, and teaching the people to produce them. That is the principal task of all Colonial Governments in all areas where there is any question of the nutritional standard being unduly low. It is, of course, essentially an educational problem, but educational in the widest sense of the word.

This does not mean that we can afford to neglect the export trade ; far from it. After all, food, indeed, even health are not the whole of life. It is impossible to be entirely happy unless you are healthy, but it does not follow that because you are healthy you are entirely happy. Actually it is hardly too much to say that moral and intellectual progress are dependent to a large extent on the export trade, not only because of the direct benefits which the individual exporter gets from the value of his exports, but also because without a healthy export trade it is only in special circumstances (as, for example, where there is entrepôt business or tourist traffic) that the Government can raise sufficient revenue to ensure adequate expenditure on the social services.

Let me here pause to sound one note of warning. Production, whether for domestic consumption or for export involves taking crops off the land year after year. You cannot go on taking out of the soil and never putting anything back. You must in all your agricultural activities and in all your development of your country's natural resources, take into account the inherent qualities of the soil. It is from the soil alone that they can draw their cheques on the Bank of Western Civilisation, and it is that alone that enables them to enjoy the benefits of the social services that we have brought to them. Unfortunately there have been too many examples throughout the Colonial Empire where the forest has ruthlessly been destroyed in order to make way for agricultural activities, when it should have been conserved to preserve the water supply or prevent soil erosion. Over and over again we find that the soil has deteriorated or become degraded owing to the faulty agricultural measures of those desiring to produce foodstuffs from it.

In most of our Colonial dependencies the local methods of the indigenous agriculture have been evolved and adapted during many generations. They suited the local needs and the social customs of the people concerned under the old conditions of life when the producers were largely independent of world trade. Circumstances have, however, greatly changed during the past fifty years, and marked environmental changes in the lives of the people concerned have resulted. Agricultural production has been stimulated, and often the need for soil conservation has been insufficiently realised. In East Africa, for example, and indeed in most of our Colonial dependencies, soil erosion problems are having to be faced. The causes for this erosion are many and varied, and it is unnecessary to go into details on this occasion. It is, however, clear that if sound development is to be achieved, steps must be taken, as indeed they are now being taken, to repair some of the damage which has already occurred and to ensure for the future that natural resources be adequately protected from waste and sound systems of agriculture be established.

The aim of all colonial administrative officers should clearly be to endeavour to secure the prosperity of the agriculturists of

G

all classes and to obtain a clear appreciation of their problems. With assistance from the various technical departments concerned, sound methods of development should be encouraged and due regard given to the need for soil conservation and the maintenance of its fertility. Considerable changes in some dependencies in the present somewhat haphazard methods of land use may be required, careful planning undertaken, and the assistance and support of the tribal organisations or native administrations secured. The problem of soil conservation is a wide one, for physical, biological and social factors have all to be given due consideration, but a beginning has already been made, and it is expected that as a result soil exploitation will be checked and a sounder agriculture developed. The proper use of land is indeed one of the most important problems of all people dependent upon agriculture for their future, and it is indeed a problem of permanent importance for our Colonial administrations.

One element in development is of course the possibility of industrialisation, and this is perhaps one of the thorniest of our problems. It is always very tempting to think that the standard of life of the community would be raised if it could make more of its own requirements itself. Specious gentlemen are always coming to us and saying that it is ridiculous to produce, say, cotton and send it right across the world to be turned into textiles and brought back again, when it could be converted on the spot ; but this argument conceals a good many fallacies. Generally speaking, small-scale production is much more expensive than large-scale. Moreover, natural aptitude plays a large part in all industrial processes, and it cannot be supposed that just anybody can operate a complicated machine. Generally speaking, our experience is that industries established in the Colonial Empire are seldom ' economic ' : that is to say, their products are seldom able to compete with imports without a very large measure of protection. There are, of course, exceptions in the Straits Settlements and Hong Kong, but there there are populations naturally well qualified for industrial work, and there are very substantial local markets and large other resources (in the Straits Settlements entrepôt and export trade ; in Hong Kong entrepôt and other similar business) to provide the local populations with money to spend on these local products. The size of these local markets is sufficient to enable the industries to establish themselves on a broad enough basis to carry on a certain amount of export trade as well. But generally speaking, I anticipate that industrialisation will be a very slow process in the Colonial Empire, and in most places I do not believe that it will ever get very far.

Our principal means of securing social development, therefore, must be to stimulate the export trade, and in particular, for the reasons which I have given above, the export trade in agricultural products. Here our principal problem is one of markets. Generally speaking, the difficulty in the Colonial Empire to-day is not to produce stuff but to sell it. Naturally we have our difficulties in connection with production and we have a very elaborate and comprehensive system of technical departments, supported where necessary with research establishments which are grappling with these problems and doing excellent work. Every year we are learning more and more of the potentialities of the Colonial Empire—what it can produce and where, and perhaps even more important, what it cannot produce in particular places. Then we have a whole series of subsidiary problems such as the problem of agricultural indebtedness, problems of land tenure and that kind of thing, but by far the biggest problem of all is that of marketing.

The old happy days when you could produce what you liked and had no difficulty in selling it, provided the quality was all right, are gone, and it will, I fear, be a long time before we shall see that state of affairs again. In some cases, but only a few, the difficulty really is that more of some particular commodity is produced than the world needs ; but in the great majority of cases the need is there all right, but quotas, exchange restrictions and other devices practised by countries which are in financial difficulties make it impossible for that need to be filled.

There are, for example, few food stuffs of greater value than citrus fruit, but except for the United Kingdom there is hardly a country in Europe where the greengrocer is allowed by his Government to import as much citrus fruit as he could sell to his customers. Citrus fruit, generally speaking, is regarded as a luxury, the importation of which must be restricted so that the Government can secure adequate supplies of goods which they

think more desirable, guns it may be in some countries, other
more innocuous objects in others.

Thus a great part of our activities are and must necessarily be
devoted to the study of markets. For certain products the
preferences which the Colonial Empire gets in the United
Kingdom and generally to a less extent in other Empire countries are of inestimable value. It is true, I think, to say that
without preference almost all Colonial sugar industries would
have ceased to exist, and I could name other Colonial products
which are almost entirely dependent on preference for their
existence.

Other great Colonial products, including rubber, which,
judged simply by the annual value of total exports is the most
important of all, get no benefit from preference. Of these products the Empire produces more than it consumes, so that preference, even where it exists, gives no price advantage. In a few
cases (rubber, tin and tea are the principal ones) salvation has
been found at any rate for the present in regulation of supply.
The principal producers of these commodities are united in an
international organisation which determines from time to time
how much of these products can safely be put on the market,
and ensures that the supplies coming forward are limited to
that amount, so that prices are kept so far as possible at a
reasonable level, neither so low as to render production un-
profitable nor so high as to discourage consumption. But for
other products, what I may call the rank and file, there is
nothing for it but close and continuous study of the market,
search for new openings, new uses and the like.

As you no doubt know, it was to grapple with this problem
that the Government recently created a new body, the Colonial
Empire Marketing Board, of which I have become Vice-
Chairman, and of which our Chairman here at this session,
Sir John Chancellor, is a member. The object of this Board is
summed up in the simple phrase " to help the Colonial Empire
to sell more and to sell it to better advantage."

And now perhaps I may look into the future. How is our
Colonial development programme going to proceed ? First, I
think we shall endeavour to develop our internal possibilities.
We shall encourage the Colonial Empire to produce more of its
own needs, more food where it needs it, and better food where

there are at present deficiencies to be made good. We shall encourage it also to produce more of its other requirements, and there may be some industrial development, but not, I think, very much.

Let me make it quite clear that we have no aspirations toward autarchy. We have no desire whatever to make either the individual Dependencies or the Empire as a whole self-sufficient. Self-sufficiency in the individual Dependency would mean in almost every case a very low standard of living. We must export as well, if we are to raise that standard. Nor can we confine our exports to the Empire. Naturally, for reasons of sentiment and because the Empire gives us the best markets, not only because of preference but also because goods sold in the Empire are sold for a free currency, we shall do our best to foster Empire trade to the utmost, but the Empire cannot in any circumstances buy all that the Colonial Empire has got to sell, and if we extend their exports we shall probably find it more rather than less necessary to develop foreign markets as well, and we fully realise that we cannot hope to sell without buying. If we sell goods to foreign countries, they can be paid for only in goods, and we can hardly under present day conditions expect to develop multilateral trade to such an extent that some other Empire country will take all the foreign goods which will thus have to be bought. Other Empire countries will, we hope, always have the first place in Colonial markets, but they cannot aspire to a monopoly.

But I feel that I must, if only to avoid future disappointment, close with a note of warning, and a warning which is, I feel sure, applicable to many other countries besides our Colonial Dependencies. In the last resort every country must live on its own resources, on what it produces and on the services it renders, whether it uses those goods or services internally or exchanges them for what it wants from other places. Some countries are rich in natural resources or have some particular aptitude for rendering services to other countries ; others have not, and the poor country cannot hope to advance as far on the road of progress as the rich country. To take an extreme case, the small coral atolls in the Gilbert and Ellice Islands which produce nothing except a few coconuts and a rather limited range of food stuffs and are separated by hundreds of miles of sea from any country with a different economic structure, can never hope to develop any great resources of wealth. We can try to help them to market their coconuts to better advantage, and we may succeed within the limits laid down by the fact that there are many other and perhaps more efficient coconut producers and there are many other products which can be used for exactly the same purposes as coconuts; but a few coconuts will never get them very far.

That of course is an extreme case, but there are many other Dependencies with a more complicated economic structure which nevertheless have been provided by Nature with resources which can never be turned to any very great advantage. For these we can and shall do our best, but whatever we do they will always be, in the last resort limited by their own poverty of resources.

I do not for a minute wish you to go away with the idea that I think that the whole Colonial Empire is made up of poor relations. That is very far from being the truth. There are still large undeveloped resources in the Colonial Empire, and although I think that under the conditions of the present day we shall over the next ten years see greater progress in the development of Colonial resources for internal use than we shall in the development of the export trade, I feel sure we shall see very real progress in the Colonial Empire.

The discussion was opened by :

Sir SELWYN GRIER[1]: We are all extremely grateful to Lord Dufferin for his address. There is one matter affecting the development of our Colonial products to which he did not refer, and that is the question of transport. At a recent Royal Empire Society luncheon I drew attention to this, as I do feel that the time has come when full enquiry should be made into the possibility of giving relief to certain parts of the Empire suffering severely from the difficulty of getting their exports to British markets at reasonable rates. It has been represented on various occasions that there is no reason why the timber from British Guiana should cost more to bring to British markets

[1] GRIER, Sir Selwyn Macgregor, C.M.G., Governor and Commander-in-Chief of the Windward Islands since 1935. Secretary for Native Affairs, Nigeria, 1921. Colonial Secretary of Trinidad, 1929–35.

than the competitive timber from the Antipodes, or that it should cost more to bring citrus fruit from Jamaica than it does from Australia.

What I want to stress to-day is that I think the whole success of the development of our Empire must depend upon our personnel. I have the greatest admiration for the way in which the selection of men for the Administrative and other services is carried out. At the present time the method of selection has been developed in such a manner that we are possibly getting the best material we can, and the training is also undertaken on very sound lines, but there is one very great danger. I think we are faced with the evil of over-centralisation. We should not continue to pile up and pile up office work on the Administrations of the Colonies, and cannot continue to do so without having a devastating effect. I speak with some feeling, because it is largely due to that reason that I am here to-day instead of being, as I should have preferred, at work in the West Indies. I have jotted down a few figures in illustration of what I am saying. The communications that came pouring into the small office of the Governor of the Windward Islands in 1930 from the Home Government were 883. In 1933 they had risen to over 1,100, and in 1936 were well over 1,900. This is rather difficult to cope with. I am touching on what I believe to be a very grave danger. I should like to see a Committee appointed to go into the question to see whether it would not be possible to cut down these returns, and so much office work, which at present is immobilising the staff. I believe the evil to be a very real one, as owing to financial stringency it often happens that in the smaller Colonies one cannot build up a big secretariat, and all this work demands that men who would be better employed in the field, getting to know the people and going about, are chained to the office stool. If something could be done to relieve that tremendous pressure which is growing at such an enormous rate, it would be a great help to the Colonies.

I agree entirely with all that Lord Dufferin has said about agricultural development. I wish that we could add cocoa as one of those industries that have been rationalised. That suggestion was made in 1933.

The development of our agricultural industries is often, and has been a great deal of late years, helped by the Institute and Imperial College, and I do hope that greater financial help will be given to the research work of the Imperial College of Tropical Agriculture. In Trinidad, largely due to this work, the production of sugar is double what it was ten years ago.

As regards personnel, might I also add this—are we not a little bit too anxious to avoid getting rid of the round peg in the square hole ? We could go too far the other way. I recently lunched with the Governor of a French Colony, who, I was credibly informed, was the thirtieth to hold office in that Colony in less than thirty years. His *chef de cabinet* informed me that the position was *très difficile* because of the seventy odd Communist Deputies in Paris. I found the Governor to be a poor, harassed little man who looked liked a Blondin posturing on an insecure tight-rope. I think we go too far in the other direction. We ought to evolve some method of shelving obvious misfits than by dumping them on one of the smaller West Indian Islands. I have only recently had a letter from a West Indian friend who said that, in his opinion, the West Indies were regarded as the ' Cinderella ' of the Colonial Empire. That sort of view has been expressed several times, and one of the reasons is that West Indians have had grounds for thinking that signs of ineptitude and inefficiency in the larger Colonies have been regarded, at times, as a passport to a West Indian appointment.

Miss PHILIPPA ESDAILE[1]: We are all exceedingly anxious for this Colonial development, but I venture to suggest that there is one factor in Colonial development that has not received the attention that perhaps it might have done—I mean the native women of the Colonies. I have had the privilege this year of visiting, as a member of the Makerere Khartoum Education Commission, Uganda and the Sudan, and I have spent the summer in St. Helena. Although my personal experience in the Colonies has been short, I think perhaps you will realise that, as I have selected this one point, it is, in my opinion, a

---

[1] ESDAILE, Miss Philippa Chichele, D.Sc., F.L.S., F.Z.S. Reader in Biology in the University of London and Head of the Biology Department, King's College for Household and Social Science. Member of the Advisory Committee on Education, Colonial Office.

vital and important matter. In these parts of the British Empire the need for the greater use of this factor in Colonial development is obvious. I have seen that the woman is really the ' primary producer ' in many places where the men would have no food at all if she did not produce it. There, it is not the custom for the men to handle the food for the household ; it is the women who select the food, till the ground, and it is the women who will make the greatest use and create the need for the products which you are hoping to encourage in the Colonies.

It is necessary to enlist the services of the women and to educate them. I was asked to meet a number of Uganda male teachers. Thirty or forty were present, and we had a great discussion about what should be the next and most important step in the forward movement, and they one and all said, " Will you not help our women ? Try to give them more education, teach them to do their own work better."

I come from King's College of Household and Social Science, where we are endeavouring to teach the women of this country to do their women's work better. It is not only the material side I have in mind, but also moral and ethical standards. If we could teach the girls in the native schools improved habits of life and methods of keeping a home, whether a grass hut or something better, I think it would be found that there will be a more general demand for a higher standard.

I paid one visit in Uganda which was of extraordinary interest. The wife had been a girl at the Gayaza High School. Her husband was a clerk in the office of the Native Administration, and she had worried her husband until he consented that their house should be of two rooms rather than one. I saw that room very nearly finished. There, work was being given to persons to make that extra room, materials were wanted for its building, and there was the possibility that better housing conditions and better moral standards could be set up in a house with two rooms instead of one.

In this endeavour to improve standards, will you not allow the women of the Empire to have better education and to be given fuller opportunities to take the part I know they should play in Colonial development ?

The VISCOUNTESS ELIBANK : I am in agreement with everything the last speaker has said about the women. A great deal might be done in the near future to help native women, to educate them, and to enable them to enjoy a better position and status in the life of their country, and so in the Empire.

There is one factor on which Lord Dufferin has not touched, but my experience in the Colonies has led me to know that the weather has an important bearing on the psychological side, I mean the human side, of development in the Colonies.

Nearly all natives foster an irrational fear of the elements, those supernatural agencies such as typhoons, hurricanes, droughts and floods, also the visitation of pests, diseases in the crops, destruction by worm or fly of fruit trees.

All these are liable to occur, and because of the effect of them upon the minds and spirits of the native populations they hinder and undermine greatly the work that is going on for the enlightenment and development of the Colonies.

Where superstition is rooted in the minds of the people progress in agriculture and in trades is slower—so I would like to remind Lord Dufferin that in all development of our Colonies and their peoples the psychological side plays a vitally important part.

Mr. C. F. Strickland[1]: Knowing the limitations of time, I want to make five points and put them briefly. I have been very interested in what Lord Dufferin and subsequent speakers have said. Let me first of all associate myself entirely with the view of one speaker that the primary producer is, in the majority of tropical countries, the woman. That is a very important matter.

The first point I want to make about the primary producer is this, that in nearly all the Colonies he or she is a small producer, a smallholder who cannot in isolation learn very easily how to produce better, and certainly cannot compete with the moneylender or the merchant with whom he or she has to deal. The first task for every Colonial Government is to remove those obstacles which have grown up through our own

[1] Strickland, Claude Francis, C.I.E., late I.C.S. Registrar of Co-operative Societies, Punjab, 1915–20 and 1922–27. Commissioner of Northern India Salt Revenue, 1921–22. Economic duty in British Malaya, 1929 ; Palestine, 1930 ; East Africa, 1931 ; West Africa, 1933   China, 1934.

action, through the introduction of a commercial economy, in the form of indebtedness or inequality in bargaining. This must be done by legislation for removal of the temptation, almost the compulsion, towards debt or towards falling into the hands of the merchant.

Secondly, these small producers, men or women, have as a rule been independent producers, not labourers, and wish to retain that status ; yet being such small producers, they cannot in isolation do anything. We have to seek a means by which they can maintain their position as independent farmers, and yet move in the international and commercial economy of to-day. That is a very important point. The independent status of the producer has to be preserved, and his independence in action extended as far as possible.

Thirdly, the Colonial Government ought in every case to adopt an active policy, not only a negative policy, as has sometimes been the case, towards bringing the small producers into larger groups where they are no longer isolated, so that they may obtain better opportunities of finance, and can deal more efficiently with the large-scale merchant, whether he be a foreigner or a swollen person of their own community. That action must be taken by the Government, because the people do not know how to do it themselves. The old tribal customs were sufficient for their former conditions of life, but we have introduced new conditions, and they have to be taught by the guiding power how to associate themselves in co-operation. That must be the active task of the Government. It is not fair for any Colonial Government to say, " By all means we have passed the law. If you associate yourselves, there is the law, and you can use it." They do not know how to use it. There must be a trained staff of teachers, of whom one or two should be overseas men, but the majority will be people from the Colony itself. They must teach the method of association for getting out of debt, association for purchase and sale—not only of goods for export, but also of products for the internal market ; this will raise the standard of living and improve the condition of the people.

Fourthly, in African colonies I have seen village after village growing one valuable vegetable, and other villages growing another valuable vegetable, whereas the right diet would contain a combination of many such vegetables and other things. There is need for teaching the men and women to grow and to buy all the things needed for the right diet within their simple domestic economy. They must be taught by persons who go into the villages, talking to the women in their own language.

My last point is this. Lord Dufferin was doubtful of the introduction of industrialisation on a large scale. If it comes, it can only come gradually, but it should not be forgotten that apart from the agriculturist in most Colonies there is also the small artisan, who is a craftsman and an artist. He is often worth preserving even though his work may have to be diverted from old purposes to something new of to-day. This transformation cannot be made by himself alone : he does not know what is wanted overseas or in the coastal towns ; he must be taught, and he will learn best if twenty or thirty artisans can be brought together. They form a co-operative association of artisans who can gradually be taught to set up a little workshop of their own. That is a true economic development of the people.

To carry industrialisation one step further, the co-operative processing of agricultural goods ought to be carried out by the people themselves. Uganda has many ginning factories, of which I believe that only one is in the hands of the people, and that is in an unstable condition. The people need skilled guidance, though not compulsion, from the Government for such objects, and a co-operative policy would have a beneficial effect.

Mr. JULIAN PIGGOTT[1]: During the opening session you will remember that in the midst of the discussion a lady got up and made one or two remarks to the following effect. She was replying to a statement which had been made regarding the decline of the birth rate within the British Empire, and she said that that decline was due in a very large degree to the all-pervading fear of war.

---

[1] PIGOTT, Julian Ito, C.B.E., M.C. Manager, British Steel Export Association since 1929. Commissioner Inter-Allied Rhine Commission, 1920–25. Member of Economic Mission to Argentine and Brazil, 1929. Member of Steel Trades Advisory Delegation, Ottawa Conference, 1932. Member of Federation of British Industries Mission to Japan, 1934.

Although those remarks were touched upon by one or two of the subsequent speakers, I make no apology for referring to them here quite shortly, and I am going to ask whether this Conference could not make some contribution to peace, because all these plans that are being made, whether for raising the standard of living or anything else, will not be of much good if the world is going to be engulfed once more in war.

I am going to take up the closing passages of Lord Dufferin's remarks to-day, in which he spoke of the need for wider export markets, and to suggest that there is a possible method which will not only be a real contribution to peace, but will also benefit the British Colonies and Dominions of the British Empire. We have heard a great deal about economic appeasement, and I wonder often whether people have clearly in mind what that means ? The first example, we are told, is a trade pact with the United States. I think everybody would heave a sigh of relief if that trade pact could be translated into something real ; but is that economic appeasement or is it not rather a political agreement ?

No doubt American motor-car manufacturers will be appeased if they have a larger market here, but I suggest that if negotiations for this trade pact were to be followed by the news that a trade pact was going to be negotiated with one of the dissatisfied powers, that would really be a step towards economic appeasement.

We have heard that there is an urgent desire to expand markets for the primary products of the Empire : we know that there are—in Europe particularly—countries where there exists to-day a much larger market for primary products, waiting to be filled. I am going to ask you to allow me to mention Germany. We are here, without rancour or bias, to consider these problems, but one often finds that if Germany is mentioned, the temperature of the room rises. I want you to consider calmly and seriously whether it would not be worth while to make a trade pact with one of the leading dissatisfied countries, who is, after all, a large potential consumer of those primary products.

I have been connnected this year with a private attempt on scientific lines to get more raw material from the Empire into Germany. The attempt has not been crowned with much

success, because we started at the wrong moment, during a
boom when farmers and producers could sell all they wanted
to at good prices. But I maintain that this question of enabling
dissatisfied countries to obtain more raw materials is at least
worthy of serious study, and only a little time ago I read in
The Times that the French Government is considering some
sort of barter arrangement with Germany in order to enlarge
the market for French Colonial products. In conclusion I would
say that if politics have decreed that an attempt shall be made
to make a trade pact with America, then politics should also
decree that an attempt be made to conclude a trade pact with
one or more of the dissatisfied powers. Let us take Germany
first, because her need is the most urgent.

Mr. ALEXANDER HOLM[1]: With that diffidence and reserve
which should characterise the remarks of a retired civil servant
on deferred pay, I must exercise care in expressing my views.

As an agriculturist I have noted the exceptional prominence
given at this Conference to the importance of agricultural
development not only in the Dominions but in the Colonial
Empire. In the Lovat Committee Report it was clearly established that the progress and prosperity of the Colonial Empire
were dependent chiefly upon its agricultural production. Yet
strange as it may seem, the policy of Colonial Governments
has not readily reacted to that conclusion, though it should be
said that since the appointment of Sir Frank Stockdale as
Agricultural Adviser to the Secretary of State, there has been
an increasing recognition of the best methods to be adopted in
creating wealth and therefore prosperity in the Colonial
Empire.

To their credit, writers on Colonial questions and persons
attending meetings of organised bodies here in London, continually urge the provision of more and more social services
for the native peoples, and almost invariably these are referred
to as increased educational facilities and improved medical
services on a large scale. Now I do not for a moment depreciate

---

[1] HOLM, Alexander, C.M.G., C.B.E. Under-Secretary for Agriculture, Union
of South Africa, 1912–19. Chairman of Wheat Commission, South Africa,
1917. Chairman of Labour Commission, Kenya, 1927. Chairman of Food
Control Board, Kenya, 1929. Chairman of Coffee and Sisal Industries Committee, 1931.

the imperative need and value of these services nor fail to mention the lamentable hygienic conditions and the very low standard of living, accompanied by malnutrition, among the native peoples, but I wish to stress the point that Governments can only provide increased social services from expanding revenues derived from production.

The world slump should have taught the lesson that industry cannot recover within itself. The great masses of population not only in the Empire, but throughout the world, are producers of primary products and, in the world's trade, increased demand for the products of industry is to a large extent dependent upon the spending power of these large masses of population.

Consumers in industrial countries complain about the rising cost of living, but I am afraid that insufficient notice is taken of the fact that they often benefit from the fact that their supplies are often marketed at below cost of production, or that the returns to native and other producers are entirely inadequate.

Mention has been made at this conference of the cost of distribution to consumers. In many cases there is a great disparity between the original cost price of primary and secondary products and their cost price to the consumer, and it would be helpful to producers if attention were given to economies in distribution costs. In fairness to retailers, much of the blame rests with the consumers on account of the demands they make for service.

Great efforts are being made in our Colonies to reduce costs of production ; the research and experimental work of past years is now bearing fruit and costs are being reduced through increased yields and the reduction of risks arising from diseases and pests.

Now let me say a word or two about ' soil erosion ' which to Commissions, Boards and Committees, is as steel to a magnet.

I do not minimise the seriousness of this question in many countries and in some of our colonies, but the impression may easily be conveyed to the minds of those who read some of the statements made that some territories will cease to produce and sustain the life of its present population. Large areas are undoubtedly seriously affected by soil erosion in one form or another, but there remain vast areas which, by virtue of their natural conditions, are the most productive and are not so damaged. In his valutalbe report on East Africa, recently published, Sir Frank Stockdale has dealt with the practical measures which should be adopted and, in the belief that Governments and individuals will take proper steps to control this evil and recondition damaged areas, there is in my judgment no reason to be unduly pessimistic about the future. In native areas administrative action can be more effectively applied than in those countries where individual ownership exists.

Appropriate reference was made yesterday to the development of ' the Imperial estate ' by Mr. Somerville. Some say that, to use an American idiom, Britishers are ' Land Poor ' and it may not be inappropriate to express some views bearing on this question. Although progress made in the development of the Colonial Empire has been impressive, the view may be fairly expressed that, with the experience now gained as to the directions in which development and production can be promoted and increased, the time has arrived for accelerating the rate of progress. The Budgetary position of our Colonies is sound and substantial reserves are being built up, but in my opinion development has for a lengthy period been too dependent upon financial provision derived from revenue accruing annually.

From the Colonial Development Fund assistance has been afforded in some important directions, but the limited means thus made available are insufficient for carrying out that large scale development which the owner of an estate might be expected to undertake on his property.

Let me give an illustration of what might be accomplished. Recently in one of our Colonies a survey was undertaken of its potential production within a reasonable time by its present population, and after making provision for its food supplies. It was found that production of the order of £1 million would result from the expenditure of about £10,000 annually on increased Agricultural Services, i.e., at a cost of 1 per cent of the value of the products. Supposing that the value of the production is halved, the cost only amounts to 2 per cent. It will be interesting to see the reaction of the Government concerned to the result of this survey. If for no other reason than that the international situation appears to demand it. Development throughout the Colonial Empire should be speeded up in every direction possible and practicable by fostering increased native production, stimulating settlement, and encouraging the employment of capital along sound lines.

Mr. A. S. HAYNES[1]: I have just returned from a Conference of all the nations of the East in Java, and this Conference has been considering the very points which we are considering here to-day. My first suggestion is that we could learn a considerable amount from studying the report which has been written as the result of that Conference.

It seems to me that Conferences multiply themselves indefinitely, but the action which is given perhaps to the most serious recommendations falls short of what is expected. In Java all the nations of the East met together, representing half the population of the world, 90 per cent of that population being agricultural. I had the privilege some time ago of being Chairman of the Preparatory Commission for that Conference, which visited nearly all the countries of the East, and I would like to urge strongly upon different administrations under the Colonial Office, the high importance of encouraging officials serving in the Colonies to visit the territories of other nations, particularly those near at hand, in order to pool experiences and learn by short cuts. Our problems in the East are common to many of the problems of the Dutch East Indies, French Indo-China, the Philippines, Siam and, of course, British India. By exchanging officials or by encouraging officers to take leave and study common questions in these territories, benefit will result to both sides. I know that this is the opinion of officials in Indo-China and the Dutch East Indies.

I would like to urge very strongly that some consideration be given to the very carefully written Report of the Java Conference. The first and most important point dealt with was that the underlying element of national stability is the soil and the man who lives on and by the soil. That has been stressed

[1] HAYNES, Alwyn Sidney, C.M.G., late Malayan Civil Service. Secretary for Agriculture, Straits Settlements and Federated Malay States, and Director of Food Production, 1922. British Adviser, Kelantan, 1930. Member of Executive and Legislative Councils, Straits Settlements, 1933.

H

here in this present discussion : if we increase the prosperity of
that man we are increasing the national income at its source.
When we do that we are, by providing increased revenue,
enabling the essential services to be carried out, so that we get a
circle on the right lines.

Nutrition cannot be tackled without staff. More money is
required. It is the same with medical services, and the importance of these services cannot be over-estimated. The man
suffering from chronic malnutrition, who is apathetic and
lethargic, cannot take an interest in the various people who try
to interest him in better agricultural co-operation and better
services. Instances of people who have by a higher standard of
living been raised to a higher standard of health are abundant.
For instance, the labourers of Southern India who are taken to
Malaya to work on the rubber estates, become entirely different
individuals, healthy, strong stout fellows, willing to rise to a
higher standard of living. The report on the Royal Commission
on Agriculture in India, 1928, strongly urged that the fundamental move to be made must be to tackle the apathy of the
peasant himself.

Another matter I would like to urge is that in the preparation
of budgets more attention should be given to rural areas. It
has been my experience in a limited sphere to see the preparation of budgets, to see them gone through, and frequently to see
this and that being struck out because it dealt with rural areas
and expenditure on inarticulate people, while money is left in
for bricks and mortar in the big towns where the people would
soon make a row in the newspapers if their requirements were
not satisfied. When retrenchment comes along, it is common
experience for it to fall more heavily upon rural than upon
urban services, and the first thing to be cut out is something
dealing with the countryside.

I recently saw a proposal to remove the capital of a certain
country from one existing town to another only fifty miles
away. These two towns are already united by a first-class road,
by a railway and by telephone. The change is to be made at a
cost of six million dollars. It seemed to me that if the administration there were fully provided with irrigation works, anti-
malarial services and medical and health staff, they might not
unwisely spend their money in that way, but until these ser-

vices were satisfied, six million dollars seemed an enormous expenditure of money.

What is needed is a re-orientation of policy which will put first things first and promote the health and prosperity of those millions who are the producers of food and raw materials and it should always be borne in mind that this can be done by a wise allocation of funds.

Sir EDWARD STUBBS[1]: I rise to thank Lord Dufferin for his very interesting and able address, which has filled me with hope that the Colonial Office is now seriously thinking of matters which it has been accused in the past of neglecting. One sentence particularly appealed to me when he said that he realised that in the case of the Colonial Empire there were not three problems but a great number. That has cheered me, because for many years my trouble has been that the Colonial Office appears to regard one Colony as just the same as another.

Sir Selwyn Grier has referred to the flood of documents on blue-grey paper in italic type, which descends on Colonial governors by every mail. These documents, containing unimpeachable sentiments expressed in faultless English, are unfortunately usually based on the theory that all Colonies are alike, and when I had the pleasure of governing Jamaica my friends in the Council used to say, " Does the Colonial Office think that we West Indians are the same as West African niggers ? "

The extent to which zeal for centralisation has obsessed headquarters is shown in the numerous schemes for the amalgamation of services which, now that I have retired from His Majesty's service, I may be allowed to describe as largely window-dressing and eye-wash. What it is necessary to realise is that the Colonies of the British Empire are not only Colonies, but in many cases old and established nations with ideas of their own which will not always fit in with those of other parts of the Empire and centralised government. I speak with some feeling, because I think it is a mistake to endeavour to deal in the same manner with the primitive populations of Africa and

---

[1] STUBBS, Sir Edward, G.C.M.G. Governor and Commander-in-Chief, Ceylon, 1933. Member of West African Lands Committee, 1912. Captain-General and Governor-in-Chief of Jamaica, 1926–32. Governor of Cyprus, 1932–33.

an ancient and civilised country such as Ceylon. Ceylon especially has suffered from the idea that Colonies should be induced to follow the example of the other parts of the Empire, and that it can be treated in the same way as the City of London. That is a belief that I have not found to be shared by any of the numerous races of Ceylon or by any individual of that race.

I have been much interested in the remarks of some speakers, especially the suggestion that women are the primary producers, and do not play the full part they should in the affairs of the State. In none of the countries that I know are women the primary producers, so far as agricultural products are concerned, but in none of them can it be said that they have little influence. People who have not lived long in the Colonies fail to understand what a tremendous amount of private pressure is exercised by women. I can assure the lady who spoke that the influence of the ordinary women in the Colonies is very much greater than it appears on paper.

I was much interested in Mr. Strickland's remarks, because one of the things I have tried to rub in for many years is the absolute necessity for co-operation and co-operative societies for the benefit of the small man who usually is not able to act for himself because he has not the means to apply his thoughts to action. I believe that the future of the Colonies is largely bound up with the progress of co-operative societies.

Mr. Haynes touched on the great importance of people from our Colonies visiting the Colonies of other great powers. If he will refer to a report which I wrote in 1910, and which was very unfavourably received by his then colleagues, he will find that I made the same suggestion there, and it was one of the things particularly objected to. The British Colonial official did not see how it was possible to learn anything from the Colonies of any other power. When I was Governor of Hong Kong, I made a suggestion on the same lines—that arrangements should be made for periodical meetings between British Governors in the East and the Governors of the neighbouring Colonies of foreign powers. I know that the only result of the suggestion was an outburst of indignation from the Secretary of State for Foreign Affairs, but I still think the idea was a good one, and I should like Lord Dufferin to give it his consideration and encouragement.

THE CHAIRMAN (Sir John Chancellor) : We are all deeply indebted to Lord Dufferin for his admirable address : it leaves one with a feeling of optimism and of confidence in the future of the Colonies.

I do not think we can measure the value of Imperial Preference to our Colonies. When I governed the Mauritius over twenty years ago, hardly a ton of Mauritius sugar came to the United Kingdom, whereas to-day, owing to Colonial preference, nearly the whole of the crop comes to England. In Trinidad the production of sugar there has more than doubled since I left. It was then 70 thousand tons, and is about 140 thousand tons to-day. When I left Southern Rhodesia nine years ago, the imports of Rhodesian tobacco into the United Kingdom amounted to about two million pounds, and to-day they are 22 million pounds in weight, and they are growing every year. These are striking examples of the benefits of Colonial preference.

Lord Dufferin has told us how difficult it is to-day for the primary producer to obtain a market for his produce, and that difficulty is universal throughout the world at the present time. I am Chairman of the Live Stock Commission which has to deal with the problem of low prices, which has caused heavy losses to our farmers of recent years. I have always felt deep sympathy with primary producers who, as Lady Elibank has told us, have to contend with tempest, diseases, droughts and floods. They have to bear the losses caused by these natural forces. They cannot often pass them on to the consumer.

At the present time the great difficulty is the disposal of products at remunerative prices. I believe that that difficulty is in a large measure brought about by the extreme nationalism which has developed in some nations to-day. I like to think that that is only a passing phase. There is little doubt that the total production of the world at present is not greatly in excess of the total needs of the population of the world. There are still many people in the world whose wants are not fully met. It is mal-distribution and shortage of purchasing power that cause the apparent excess. When the peaceful outlook, of which Mr. Julian Piggott held out hopes, can be achieved, there should be great improvement in the adjustment of supply and demand throughout the world.

The nutrition of the people is a very important question. There is much to be done in studying it and much to be learned. I have been told that the mineowners in the Belgian Congo have for some time given great attention to this matter. They have found that the labourers whom they recruit on arrival at the mines are usually suffering from under-nourishment and not fit for heavy work. It is their practice to give the new labourers three months of an ample diet and light labour before putting them on heavy work underground. I hope that His Majesty's Government will give special attention to this subject as one of great importance, not only in the Colonies, but also in this country.

I agree with much that Mr. Strickland has said. I had the advantage of having his services in Palestine, where he came to make a report upon the possibility of establishing co-operative credit-banks in that country. Long before that I had contact with this question in Mauritius. Co-operative credit-banks were established there twenty-five years ago, and they were very successful. It is interesting to observe that their success depends largely upon the racial aptitude of the people concerned. Among Indians in India and elsewhere co-operative credit-banks have been a great success. Among the negro races they are not as a rule successful. When they were started in Palestine, they did not succeed among the Arabs. But of course one must remember that instruction and close supervision are necessary in introducing ideas of co-operation among primitive peoples. The Jews, on the other hand, took to co-operative credit-banks with enthusiasm, and they established co-operative credit organisations in connection with almost every activity. In fact, they almost overdid it. They required no teaching to make co-operative credit banks a success.

Mr. Julian Piggott referred to the advisability of more British capital being put into the British Colonies. I should like to reinforce that suggestion. I submit that British capital would be safer if invested in developing the resources of British Colonies than lent to some of the foreign states which do not pay their debts.

Sir Edward Stubbs referred to the advantages to be gained from visits to foreign Colonies : that is an admirable suggestion.

In conclusion I desire to thank Lord Dufferin for his most interesting address

I am sure that I am expressing your views when I say we all specially welcome him both as Under-Secretary to the Colonies and also as the grandson of that very distinguished statesman, Lord Dufferin, Viceroy of India. I hope that in the career on which he is setting out he will render equally great services to the Empire. On behalf of all here I offer Lord Dufferin our sincere thanks.

Sir ARCHIBALD WEIGALL : I wish to offer one word of thanks to Sir John Chancellor for presiding. May I also say what a tremendous joy it is to welcome Lord Dufferin. When he was asked by the Society, of course the office he holds was taken into consideration, but it was really due to the fact that from the time he went to Eton he has shown brilliant promise, which has so early matured into brilliant performance, and we were determined to get hold of him as soon as possible.

May I also say that we are extremely grateful to the whole of the hierarchy of the Colonial Office. The Under-Secretary, the Permanent-Secretary and Agricultural Adviser are here, and they have been extremely kind to us, as were the officials of the Dominions Office yesterday.

On the subject dealt with in this session I was much struck with what Sir Selwyn Grier said about personnel. A short time ago I went round the West Indies on behalf of the Royal Empire Society and was extraordinarily impressed by the huge amount of responsibility placed upon our British administrators throughout the West Indies. I also saw some cases where it was obvious that there was a square peg in a round hole. I mentioned this on my return and invariably the answer was, " Yes, but dear old So-and-so has only two more years to run for his pension." That is all very well, but we are not fulfilling our trust as trustees of the Empire if we allow duds to remain one single day in office.

IV

THE PROBLEM AND THE WORLD

Wednesday, November 24th. Afternoon Session

Sir GEORGE SCHUSTER[1] in the Chair : It is my pleasant duty
to introduce to you to-day Sir John Wardlaw Milne. I need
not waste any time in dealing with Sir John's qualifications,
which are so well known to you, and as he has chosen, or had
put upon him, " The Problem and the World " to deal with,
I think he will probably require every minute that is available
to deal with it ; therefore I shall take no more of your time,
but will ask Sir John to address you.

Sir JOHN WARDLAW-MILNE[2]: The object of this Conference
is fully set out in the Agenda, and you have already had very
valuable contributions dealing with the position between this
country and the Dominions, with India and with the Colonies.
I have been asked to try and put before you the World Problem,
and I need hardly say that I approach such a task with much
diffidence and trepidation.

It is, I think, not too much to say that the whole world
situation in trade and prosperity was radically altered by the
Great War. In many parts of the world customary production
had ceased, and in those countries not actively engaged in the
conflict a level of unnatural and inflated prices existed. At the
close of the War new frontiers were established, new barriers
to trade created, and old markets disappeared. The harmony

---

[1] SCHUSTER, Sir George, K.C.S.I., K.C.M.G., C.B.E., M.C. Financial Secretary to Sudan Government, 1922–27. Economic and Financial Adviser, Colonial
Office, 1927–28. Finance Member of Executive Council of the Viceroy of India,
1928–34.

[2] WARDLAW-MILNE, Sir John, K.B.E., M.P. (Unionist) for the Kidderminster
Division of Worcestershire since 1922. Member of Bombay Municipal Corporation, 1907–17. Additional Member of the Legislative Council of the Governor
of Bombay and of the Council of the Governor-General of India. President of
Government of India's Advisory Shipping Committee. Member of the Imperial
Economic Committee, 1926–29.

between agricultural lands, the sources of raw materials, and the industrial countries, as exporters of manufactured goods was completely upset by unnatural boundaries. The position of debtor and creditor was altered, barter was re-established, and self-sufficiency was the goal, with governmental interference and control an ever-growing phenomenon.

To a large extent these altered conditions were imposed by political necessity, and although nearly twenty years have passed, the internal situation of many nations is still governed by the results of the War, and they have not yet begun, or are only now beginning, to emerge from the strangling conditions of that period. Particularly is that so in Central Europe, and there, as elsewhere, apart from anything else, political action is essential to restore normal conditions of trade.

From the point of view of world prosperity, perhaps the worst feature of this situation is the search for self-sufficiency, the conception that every country should seek independence by the production of its own necessities, even if at a heavy cost in inferior or substitute goods, and this, behind an impenetrable hedge of tariffs, prohibitions and currency restrictions. Primarily this conception is of a military character and is largely governed by strategic considerations. But we have to face the fact that it exists, and the road to the reversal of this scheme of supercharged nationalism—which in itself is more likely to lead to fresh wars than otherwise—is likely to be a long one upon which advance will only be made by slow stages and by international political action and good-will.

The course of world trade has been severely affected by the slumps of 1921–22 and 1930–31, the complete abandonment of the old gold-exchange standard, the inflation and depreciation of currencies, and the practical bankruptcy of several important consuming nations. It would take much too long to deal fully with these events here, and indeed it is unnecessary to do so, for their effect upon the prosperity of the world is well known and understood. No comparison with pre-War conditions is of real value either, for statistics are rendered almost useless for this purpose owing to the changes in money and values. I pass therefore to the basis of the year 1929, which is looked upon as a good trade year, and will endeavour to give a picture, however imperfect, of the changes since that date.

In that year the value of world trade was estimated to be £14,100,000,000 in terms of gold. In subsequent years it fell steadily to the lowest point of £7,747,000,000 in 1933–34, since when it had slowly improved to £8,710,000,000 in 1936. The figure is likely to be higher still for 1937, but even so, is not likely to reach anything like the total of 1929. The outstanding feature of this 15 per cent rise since 1933 is the increase in the turnover of raw materials and manufactured goods, which accounts for much the largest part of it, the quantum of food-stuffs being actually lower in 1936 than in 1933. As the recent improvement also is greater in base metals and raw iron than in purely manufactured goods, the indications point conclusively to the requirements of armament production throughout the world. In this connection it may be interesting to record that the level of world armament expenditure last year, on a gold basis, was three times that of 1913 and twice that of the average 1924–30.

The British Commonwealth's share in world trade fell from 27.9 per cent in 1929 to 26.7 per cent in 1931, but has since increased to 31 per cent. The United Kingdom's share of world trade is now 14.5 per cent, but our recent improvement is entirely due to increased imports in 1936, our share of world exports having actually fallen in that year.

The share of the United States in the world's trade is 11.2 per cent, Germany 8.59 per cent, France 5.82 per cent, Canada 3.95 per cent, Japan 3.67 per cent, and Belgium 3.28 per cent. These seven countries between them do, therefore, over 50 per cent of the trade of the world, and no other single country reaches as much as 3 per cent. I hope my subsequent remarks will make clear to you why I have inflicted these statistics upon you here.

In most countries the declaration made by Empire represen-tatives after the abortive World Economic Conference, to the effect that a substantial rise in the price level was of the greatest importance and a prime object of international statesmanship, is fully concurred with. Let us see therefore what has been achieved in this direction, bearing in mind that most economists have agreed that at least the level of 1929 must be secured and maintained. Taking some countries which may be said to have made, comparatively, a considerable advance in recovery, we find, on the basis of 1929= 100, that in Australia, at the end of last year, the level of wholesale prices was only 84, against 79 in 1933 ; in Sweden 90, against 78 ; in Japan 97, against 79 ; in the United States 88, against 74, and in the United Kingdom 88, against 76. It will be seen, therefore, that there is still some distance to go to reach the 1929 level, and I may add that in this country we are not only to-day 10 per cent below that figure, but 20 per cent below the beginning of the century, which was about the lowest period for 150 years.

In the years after the War we supported a general price level 40 per cent over 1913, with a world production lower than it had been for years, while to-day we are little above 1913, and much below the average of 1850–80.

The other important recommendation was the necessity for stability in international currencies and freedom in exchange, and hardly a month has passed since without speeches from the statesmen of one or other country emphasising the vital importance of these questions.

I am much tempted to indulge in a retrospective survey of the course of events in connection with the currency of our own country since the War, but I realise that such is not my task to-day. But certain facts I must deal with. I would remind you that the grave defects of the old gold standard were really hidden in pre-War days by new discoveries of the metal, with the result, for example, that the gold output of the world from 1903 to 1913 was four times that of 1880–90, with a corresponding increase in the prosperity level. In 1920–23 a deflation of currency, in my opinion, was deliberately engineered (upon the advice of what I can only call a ' Moneylenders' Committee ') whereupon wholesale prices dropped in 1921 to 60 per cent of the previous year's level, and to 50 per cent in 1922–23. In 1925 we re-committed ourselves to the old gold standard, for what reason I have never been able to understand, with the usual result that a fall in prices ensued, at an accelerating rate, to touch bottom in 1931 at 60 per cent below the 1924 level.

Since we were ignominiously forced off gold in 1931, in circumstances which I trust will never be repeated in the history of this country, prices, as I have pointed out, have been maintained, or rather better than maintained, but we have a long way to go to get back to 1929, and still further to reach the prosperity levels of 1924.

I turn now to another aspect of this part of the problem, and that is the variation in values of the currencies of the different countries. Although these show wide differences measured in gold, there is one bright aspect of the matter, and that is that, while all are not effectively adhered to, fluctuations in recent years have not been of an extreme character, rarely exceeding 3 per cent in the years 1929 to 1936. That there are wide differences measured in gold is evident, however, when I record that the percentage of the 1929 value in the case of the United States is 59, Belgium 72, France 65, United Kingdom 60, Argentine 45, Japan 34 and Russia 22.

As you all know, the creation of the Sterling Area, and the Tripartite Agreement have been of immense benefit, and for this and for the inauguration of Exchange Equalisation Accounts, we owe a deep debt of gratitude to our present Prime Minister and to the officials of the British Treasury. The avowed object is to maintain the greatest possible equilibrium in the system of international exchanges, and that is eminently desirable indeed, although it must never be subordinated to the still more important goal of an increased and stable level of prices. The latter object will go far to secure, while the former alone will not attain, the safeguarding of peace and the promotion of prosperity throughout the world.

At the same time the setting up of these Equalisation Funds, and particularly the close co-operation which their successful working demands, between the financial authorities in the different countries, is of great value in bringing about that stability which alone makes it possible for international trade to move along well-oiled channels. It is the loss of the standard of value throughout the world that has been one of the main causes of our discontents, and until we recover it, we shall have neither security nor prosperity. We can never again agree to be dependent upon the out-turn of gold, which a few years ago was in a very short supply and which at the moment, owing to Russia's production, is again coming forward in increasing quantities. No feasible method of redistributing the large stock—the greater part of that existing—in the hands of two or three nations has yet been discovered, and our future monetary policy, while possibly continuing the use of gold in its place, and silver also I hope, must be independent and capable of at all time supplying the increasing population and improving trade with every possible facility they may require. The value of our money must rest on the real wealth of the country, our food production, factories, ships and docks, and not upon the chance output of any metal.

I would only here add that to me the time has come for Great Britain, which gave the lead in these measures, so valuable to date, to go further now and take the next step in the setting up of an Exchange Pool for the Empire and the Sterling Area, upon which all Central Banks can freely operate to facilitate still further the free exchange of their productions and to provide security in value for his goods and his labour both for the merchant and the producer. I have dealt with this proposal on other occasions, and will therefore refrain from elaborating it further here. But the fact that a large proportion of the World's trade is carried on by a few countries shows the immense power which they have to start an upward movement.

The main objective, then, to ensure world prosperity, is a substantial rise in the price level, and stability at that level when we have secured it. In manufacturing countries, such as this, a heavy fall has not the same dire effect, at first at any rate, as in purely agricultural communities, for with a drop in prices the manufacturer can purchase his raw materials on a more favourable basis, and thus, to some extent, meet the decline in the selling values of his output. But in agricultural countries, which, speaking roughly, include the greater part of the Empire, a drop in prices is disastrous, for if it be, to the extent of 50 per cent for example, twice as much of his produce has to be given by the agriculturist to obtain the money required for taxes, interest and purchases of manufactured goods. As between 80 and 90 per cent of the population of the world are producers, and 60 per cent of it engaged in agriculture, it is not difficult to understand the terrible consequence of the last slump from which the world suffered. A fall in prices is merely, in other words, an appreciation in the value of money, and the two problems, therefore, price level and currency management, are inseparably bound together.

There is, however, one last aspect of the matter which I must mention, although, as you will hear it fully discussed at a subsequent session, I shall not deal with it in detail. It is the problem of production and consumption. I have never believed that there is such a thing as over-production, although there well may be a temporary glut of one or more commodities. But under-consumption exists, as we know only too well, and there will be no outstanding prosperity throughout the world until we bring back to all peoples the power to buy and provide for those who have never had enough a standard of living which ensures comfort and increased consuming power.

It is generally agreed that normally the population of the globe increases by between 1 and 2 per cent per annum. On this basis, the world had to cater for an increase of say 10 per cent since 1929, but, as I have previously shown, the world trade in foodstuffs has actually declined in that period. Nor, if we take the great basic crops of the world, do we find any increase in recent years to cause anxiety as to consumption. In the years 1930–31 to 1936–37 the total cotton crop of the world was 196 million bales, and the consumption 183½ million, leaving a surplus only equal to five months' requirements. In wheat, in eleven years from 1926–27 to 1936–37, the world's production (including Russia's exports) was 39,272,000 bushels, and the consumption 39,364,000. In barley, maize, jute and a number of other commodities similar figures could be given. The world is well able in normal times climatically to produce all and more than all that is necessary for human requirements. There will be shortages occasionally and bumper crops in their season. Perhaps the lesson of the seven fat and the seven lean years was not only for Biblical days, but for all time, and the example of Joseph might well be followed by modern statesmanship. One possible danger, however, in the consideration of consumption in the future should be noted. An increase of purchasing power without securing that the people themselves produce more wealth may lead to disaster. Such a course will not solve the world's economic problem. It merely leads to loss of confidence and the withdrawal of capital. I fear both France and America may have erred in this way, and we ourselves are not entirely free from suspicion.

To sum up, then—as I see it, the problem for the world, is primarily one of consumption, which in its turn means an increasing standard of life and comfort for all peoples. To secure this, the main essential is the raising of the price level to give the producers, and particularly the agriculturist—by no means forgetting our much-neglected agricultural industry here at home—a real return for his labour. No such rise, however, will be secure without a widening co-operation in currency management and the re-establishment of a world standard of value. Then will come the provision of that capital which is essential for increased prosperity and which in our case is also necessary for the promotion of migration, without which parts of our Empire may soon be in real and serious danger. Empire and foreign lending, however, valuable as it is, should never overshadow the vital need for capital for our own agriculture, to replace the constant drain which has taken place in this country during the last half-century.

These measures will only have their influence in certain countries when their rulers realise that to carry propaganda to the length of keeping their people ignorant of real world conditions in the supposed interests of self-sufficiency is retarding all recovery. It is merely a sign of fear and really betrays an inferiority complex.

The problems are not all economic, unfortunately—they are also largely political. No country can be really prosperous by itself. Distance has been destroyed and frontiers will be more and more difficult to maintain. We are facing a new world with great problems, but even greater opportunities. Science offers us a larger and fuller life with much of human toil removed and replaced by leisure and opportunity for all. How are we going to use them ? Our progress seems painful and halting, and the world is wasting valuable time and money on its vast and useless expenditure on arms, which in itself continually delays our journey forward.

In spite of the difficulties I, for one, believe that slowly but surely the darkness is passing, and that we are approaching that brighter dawn of world co-operation and peace which lies ahead.

Sir GEORGE SCHUSTER : We have had such a number of subjects of great importance put before us that it will be difficult to keep the discussion on well-focussed lines. It is my task now to throw the meeting open to discussion, but the Secretary has asked me before doing so to make a few remarks of my own. I do so with the greatest diffidence because I see present here to-day distinguished gentlemen who can speak with a good deal more authority than I can on a number of subjects. But I will try to make a small contribution as to the way in which the discussion might go.

I am sure we are all here with a practical purpose in our minds, therefore, as far as possible, I am sure we should all desire at this Conference to suggest measures which are practicable and can achieve something tangible in the future. If I might venture to put up a point of view which might lead to a discussion on the lines on which Sir John has opened the subject, I would like to say this. I entirely agree with a great deal of what he said on the economic side : I particularly strongly agree with what he said about the necessity of a rising price level if we are really to have a period of world prosperity. I happen to have taken, as delegate for India at the Ottawa Conference, a part in framing those currency resolutions to which Sir John referred, and I often look back upon them and think that they were well framed. It seems to me that many statesmen who started on the course of price raising, seem to have been frightened at the success of their own efforts, and that part of our trouble to-day has been not only the lack of methods for controlling the rising tendency when once started, but also a lack of confidence in the rightness of the objective. I think perhaps that in the United States we may see a particularly clear example of that.

Having expressed agreement on that particular point, I would venture to say that I think Sir John may be said to have dealt with this matter rather too much on purely economic lines. He did at the end say that of course the questions were not only economic but also political. I think the political side is of major importance to-day, and that—whatever may have been their origin—it is political objectives pursued for their own value that are increasing economic difficulties. Let me try to illustrate that. He mentioned self-sufficiency ; exaggerated self-sufficiency is a terribly mistaken policy. But have we any of us considered how much we ourselves contributed towards the justification of a policy of self-sufficiency by our own abortive attempt to apply economic sanctions as a means of controlling the policy of another country? That is a matter which deserves our serious consideration, and that is a political issue. We believe in this country largely in the ideal of a League of Nations. So do I, if it is effective, but there is terrible danger now of an ineffective League—ineffective because it does not represent a universal public opinion among nations—and of members of this limited League thinking that there has fallen upon them the moral duty of acting as Head Prefects of the world, and of using their economic power as an instrument for imposing not only their ideals of morality but also their policy upon others. That is a point we should consider, and let us consider further this policy of self-sufficiency.

I agree with Sir John that in the world to-day there is not really a problem of over-production, but a more serious problem of mal-adjustment between production and consumption, but the point I want to make is that this economic problem is being gravely aggravated by the political policies of particular countries.

Sir John gave us some very interesting figures about wheat. Wheat is one of those examples where political policies have gravely interfered with the working of economic courses. In the five years up to 1928, the three large wheat importing countries of Europe were France, Germany and Italy, and they imported on an average during those five years 211 million bushels of wheat. Since then they have, as a result of their policy of agricultural protectionism and self-sufficiency, put themselves in such a position that—given normal harvests—they no longer require imports, but might actually have a margin of wheat for export. When we are faced with a sudden disturbance of that kind, it is no good saying that in thirty years' time wheat consumption will have increased to a certain amount, because we are up against an immediate problem that upsets the equilibrium of a number of countries. What can we do to create a political situation that will make it possible for us to tackle economic problems on their own merits? That is the problem that lies before us. To throw out one idea, I believe that our best practical course is first of all to promote a very intimate and close understanding between those countries in the world who still trust each other sufficiently to believe in

I

international trade as a sane method of operation, say, the whole of the sterling area (which covers the British Commonwealth), the Scandinavian countries, France, Belgium, Holland, South America and the United States.

Let us have a very close understanding in that group, and in the unity of that closer understanding let us try to face facts honestly with the other countries and offer them a real opportunity of co-operation. That means going very wide in certain directions, really facing their problems and making an honest attempt to meet them. Whether these efforts will be met with a full response or not is another proposition, but at any rate we shall have made the attempt, and if it fails we shall be left with the strength of our own co-operation. That might serve as a suggestion for discussion and as an illustration of the point I wished to make on the relation between political and economic issues to-day.

The discussion was opened by :

Mr. PHILIPS PRICE[1]: I rise with some diffidence to open the discussion this afternoon in view of the gentlemen who are present, and who are experts on this particular subject. I have been asked to speak early in view of the fact that I have to get away to the House of Commons shortly, and I would like first of all to say how greatly I appreciate the invitation of the Royal Empire Society to some of us who are not actually Fellows, to come and take part in the discussion. We belong to different political groups in this country, and we are all invited here to put our ideas in the common pot and try to thrash out a common policy for this tremendous problem. What little contribution I can give to-day I hope will be constructive along the lines I have suggested.

Sir John in his most interesting address opened on a very sound note. He referred to the great danger in the world to-day of this idea of self-sufficiency. A short time ago I was at the Paris Exhibition and I spent some considerable time in the German exhibit and came out feeling rather depressed. I saw all the energy and the ability which German scientists and

---

[1] PRICE, Morgan Phillips. M.P. (Labour) for the Whitehaven Division of Cumberland, 1929–31. Correspondent of the *Manchester Guardian* in Russia, 1914–18, and of the *Daily Herald* in Berlin, 1919–23. Landowner and farmer.

technicians seem to be able to devote towards the production of goods in their own country, artificial products which they might be buying from Australia, British Crown Colonies and India, obviously aiming at the production of these goods themselves in order to make Germany a great self-supporting country. That seems to me to be a very grave danger, but is it altogether only Germany that is at fault ? I think there are other countries throughout the world who have been following along the same lines. Germany is the extreme example. I think it is the case of the beam and the mote : it may be that the beam is in Germany's eye, but I am not so sure that we have not a mote in our own eyes. We, too, have fallen to some extent for the idea of self-sufficiency, not so badly perhaps, but there have been schools of political thought in this country that have aimed at making the British Empire self-sufficient. I know it is impossible, but there are tendencies even now, and one of the great problems before the Empire to-day is that, given our existing economic principle here based on the Ottawa treaties, to widen and expand them so that they shall not become a hindrance to the extension of world trade. That is why I am so glad to think that the Government have taken steps with the United States to open up discussions for an Anglo-American treaty. Let us not confine ourselves to that : let us see what other countries we can bring into a low tariff scheme. I do not believe that we can go back to the old Free Trade days of Bright and Cobden, but I do believe in regulated trade, regulated by the Government in the interest of the consumers and the producers as well. I agree that the producers must have a price for their raw materials. That is one of the troubles. The primary producers have not had, and have not now, sufficient to cover their costs of production. I am inclined to agree with the Chairman. Sir John stressed the purely financial currency side of this problem. Important as I believe it is, there are other political questions involved. I have hinted at one, the trend of self-sufficiency and the need for the British Empire to take a lead in this way of opening up world trade.

The British Empire is a League of Nations within the greater League of Nations, and I am not prepared to take the view that the League of Nations should be just a discussion club dealing only with opium and the white slave traffic, not even to have the opportunity or power to deal with the major issues involved in the creation of the world international law, or to face up against those dissatisfied States who, I am afraid, are trying to create international anarchy. The problem in the immediate future is how to deal with these States, and the Empire should take the lead.

It is not enough for us to resist aggression with force. I agree with the lady who said that the women of this country cannot be expected to bear children if there is constant fear of war and of their children becoming cannon fodder. I understand that point of view ; at the same time I think the Empire must take such steps to defend itself against those who are seeking international anarchy to obtain their ends.

But that is not enough. We have to make some definite effort to extend the trade of the Empire, and to include other countries in a low tariff group. I want to stress what Mr. McDougall said at the first session, that the Empire must set an example to the world as a high standard of living group of nations. The daughters have grown up and got their own households, and have set us a good example of a high standard of living : we have to see that our Crown Colonies will follow that lead. As we heard in an interesting discussion on the Colonial Empire, we have to see that the natives for whom we are trustees in Africa, the Malay States and elsewhere, are brought up to a higher standard of living along their own lines, and not just along the lines of what we may think is desirable. We must try and find out what they want, give them what they can understand, give them what is good in our civilisation, and try to encourage them to leave what is bad in their own. If the Empire comes to be regarded as a high-living group of countries I think we can then form an example to those dissatisfied states, and persuade them to come along. I believe they will in the long run, if given the chance, and if we show them that we will not put up with aggressive tactics.

In regard to raw materials, Empire Boards have been set up to control international products, tea and tin. Why not let the dissatisfied States also have their representatives there as consumers ? It is necessary to " think big " in this matter. They may take it at once, or they may still go on with their tactics, but if we show them that we will offer them that in one hand, and a gun to resist their aggression in the other, I believe their aggression will fade away.

Sir ALAN ANDERSON[1]: Sir John was rather apologetic when he started about the title being too wide, but I think the title states the problem. We are not able to deal with world trade in watertight compartments. It is a world problem of stability and trade. The circle has been broken, and we have to mend it. We have to frame our Empire and world policy to bring that great objective about. I do not believe there is any difference between us about the target at which we aim. There has been no opposition. Everyone has said the same thing from different angles. The difficulty is how to reach it, and it does appear to me from hearing a good many discussions that we are apt to be too negative. In our foreign policy, for example, I think we have interested ourselves too much in preventing evil and discouraging nations from going to war and having arms, and too little in making peace attractive.

Someone mentioned sanctions. The League of Nations made the mistake of being too negative. That attitude does not serve in dealing with a proud nation ; I think we should be positive, and the positive appeal for peace to the world should be through trade. Those who have power to appease the nations through trade are a comparatively small number of nations. We are one, the United States is another. The nations of the British Empire have not the slightest idea of being an exclusive group, and it is to my mind vitally important to get the United States in because they are the largest creditor nation. It is essential that they should buy enough from the world to keep the exchanges right. That being the problem, it appears to me that steps are already being taken. The great creditor nations of the world got together months ago to try and stabilise the currency. This was a necessary first step and they have not been 100 per cent successful, but one step cannot be taken by itself. The trade of the world is needed to keep the currency stable, and world trade has not yet been encouraged to move.

[1] ANDERSON, Sir Alan Garrett, G.B.E. M.P. (Conservative) for the City of London since 1935. Director of Anderson, Green and Co., Ltd., Managers of the Orient Line. Director of L.M.S. Railway, the Bank of England and the Suez Canal Company. President of the Association of Chambers of Commerce 1934–5.

Money has to be stabilised, debts have to be adjusted so that the countries burdened with heavy debts can enter into trade again, and fears—political, monetary and commercial—have to be calmed. The same group of countries, and only they, can give the world a lead in all these directions. Someone accused Sir John of being too commercial. I am sometimes accused of the same thing. But our object is peace ; whether we are commercials or not, we want peace. We cannot progress until we convince the world that to murder our neighbour is the stupidest thing in the world. We are buying gas masks in the belief that someone may go mad at any moment, and we may be plunged into war. We have to get the idea across that it is just as stupid for one nation to murder its neighbour and best customer as it would be for Kent to murder Middlesex.

We have to push forward on a great campaign of propaganda, and we need not be afraid even if we have to give up something. We shall not get peace or commerce or all the advantages flowing from science and progress unless we start the world moving forward without exaggerated fears, but helping each other towards peace by the road of trade.

SIR PATRICK HANNON :[1] I do not think that we could have had a more interesting paper on all the circumstances involved in the world trade problems than we have had from Sir John Wardlaw-Milne at this Session.

You, Mr. Chairman, said at the close of your interesting commentary on his address that politics and economics were more or less inextricable in the solution of this grave question. That, I think, is a commonplace. In this country since the War our statesmen have made every effort to make our contribution to the easier flow of international trade. It will be recalled that in the first Socialist administration the then Chancellor of the Exchequer and the President of the Board of Trade made it part of their definite policy with the support of

[1] HANNON, Sir Patrick, K.B.E. M.P. (Unionist) for the Moseley Division of Birmingham since 1921. Chief Organiser, Irish Agricultural Organisation Society, 1896–1904. Director of Agricultural Organisation to the Government of Cape Colony, 1905–9. Deputy-Chairman of Birmingham Small Arms Company, Director of many companies, Member of the Executive Committee of the Federation of British Industries. Vice-Chairman of the Central Chamber of Agriculture.

their Cabinet, to endeavour to open the doors of those nations where economic nationalism had run mad, in order to make trade flow more freely. You will recall the Economic Conference at Geneva where all the European nations sent delegates to discuss this question of making possible a more facile flow of international trade, and to consider self-sufficiency from the point of view of its grave economic influence upon each of the new communities that sprang up after the War. The whole matter was examined with great care. Subsequent to that very important Conference attempts were continuously made by the British Government to invite European countries to accept the conclusions of the Conference, which all aimed at the freer movement of international trade. As is well known, not a single nation in Europe, in a greater or less degree responded to that suggestion.

In discussing this question of international trade, we must remember that we are a low tariff country, and when it is suggested that we should broaden the operation of the Ottawa Conference agreements, this question would have to be examined with very considerable care.

I contend that the first obligation of British statesmen should be the maintenance of the employment of our own people in this country and the maximum opportunities for people in the British Empire. I cannot conceive any interference with the Ottawa agreements without bringing into play forces that may have a very serious effect upon the present hopeful economic situation of this country. Our moderate protective policy in this country is the lowest tariff policy in the world. While the facts given by Sir John and the ultimate criticisms from Sir George Schuster are worthy of grave consideration by statesmen in this country, we ought to move cautiously and warily before departing from our present policy, having regard to the masses of people in this country who have to depend for their living upon the present system.

Our export trade has substantially improved, our oversea trade agreements have given an immense help to the broadening of international trade in Europe. I think we cannot go further in that broadening policy unless we have more generous concessions made to us in the process of give and take in the enlargement of these agreements. I am all in favour of the

Anglo-American trade agreement becoming one of the dominant facts of our time, but if it means that we are going to open more widely the doors of this country to the influx of American manufactured goods on the vast scale of mass production which obtains in the highly-organised condition in that country, I am bound to say that we are facing a problem that may land this country in economic difficulties as grave as those through which we passed in 1931.

I am entirely in favour of all the machinery and effort of British statesmanship being employed in the expansion of trade. No single man has concentrated more thought upon this matter than our present Prime Minister, but I am bound here, as one interested in manufacturing enterprises and also in the prosperity of agriculture, to say that we have to walk with caution, and while general principles are very acceptable on their own, the important fact is how to keep our people employed, in the enjoyment of the highest standard of living and at the highest level of production.

That is my attitude towards this most interesting, illuminating and inspiring paper. I am a humble representative in the House of Commons, but I have been associated with industry for many years, and while I am prepared to support schemes for making world trade move very freely, at the same time my first duty must be to consider the interests of our own people.

Professor NORMAN BENTWICH[1]: I must ask your forbearance if I speak on an aspect of the subject entirely outside that on which the first speaker and the Chairman indicated that the discussion might go. I wish to say a word upon the relation of the Empire to the world problem of population, and to consider, not so much the commerce of goods and movement of currency as the commerce of men and the movements of humanity. That is a very important aspect of the Empire in its relation to the world, which also affects conditions of world peace. One of the outstanding factors of our Empire is its huge size. The British Empire is nearly as great as the three next biggest Empires in the world—The United States, the Soviet Union, and

---

[1] BENTWICH, Norman, O.B.E., M.C. Professor of International Relations in the University of Jerusalem. Formerly Attorney-General to the Palestine Government.

the French Empire put together. While in parts of the British Empire there is a large mass of population, there are large parts in which the ratio of population is lower than anywhere in the world. These are found in the Commonwealth of Australia, the Dominion of New Zealand and the Dominion of Canada. Great spaces which are pre-eminently fit for the settlement of white people are to-day glaringly unpopulated in comparison with the rest of the world. An aspect of this question which does require consideration is the danger of self-sufficiency, not in trade, but in reference to humanity and races of population. The tendency has been marked in recent years for the British Empire to put a restriction on the migration of other than British people into the Empire. That is a danger to the Empire itself, and it is one of the deeper causes of world unrest. It is of that I wish to say a word, particularly in regard to my own people, the Jews.

The Jewish people to-day are passing through a period of terrible stress, particularly in Central Europe. We are faced to-day with this terrible persecution of the Jews in Germany, and with an equally terrible persecution in Poland. In those countries there is a population seeking a home in some land where it can be free to develop its powers and capacities ; and the countries of the British Empire are above all those to which the Jews would turn if the doors were open.

I have spent the greater part of the last twenty years in Palestine, and have seen a remarkable development of the country by the Jewish people. That country which before the War was neglected and backward, although it is passing through, at the moment, troubled political circumstances, has reached a stage of economic prosperity and general well-being which amazes all who have seen it. That has been brought about to a great extent by the immigration there of Jews from Central Europe. The Jews coming there have turned to the simple productive occupations with which the world in general does not generally associate them, tilling the soil and cultivating the land.

The Jewish population has grown in the last twenty years from 50,000 to over 400,000, and a large part of those people are living on the soil in villages.

In Germany and in Poland, and other countries of Central and Eastern Europe thousands of young Jews are looking for

the opportunity to emigrate and to find freedom and opportunity
to work. From Germany alone, since 1933, 130,000 have emigrated. Of that number nearly 50,000 have gone to Palestine,
but thousands would go to the British Dominions to develop
there if the conditions of immigration were easier. There has
been a small emigration to South Africa, but when less than
2,000 had gone in, there was an outcry in that country. A few
hundred have been able to go to Australia.

I suggest that our Empire must encourage a white population
which cannot be found from the British Isles, because there is
scarcely any emigration of young persons from this country ;
and therefore it should encourage and assist the settlement of
elements from other countries of Europe who can bring qualities
of industry, intelligence and loyalty, and be absorbed in the
framework of the Empire. The Jewish people in Germany and
Poland are a population of that kind. In regard to population
as well as to the treatment of the native peoples in the Empire,
and to trade and making available raw materials, we are
trustees for civilisation and not simply trustees for the British
people. We should offer a home for people who are looking for
the possibility of leading an upright and industrious life, who
may enjoy in the British Empire, as nowhere else, conditions
of fair treatment and tolerance, and who will bring gifts which
the British people would acknowledge that they have had from
the Jewish settlers in a former century.

I hope there may be some consideration of that aspect of
Empire by the Society on some other occasion.

Mr. MUNRO ROGER asked leave to put a correcting question
on the remarks of Professor Bentwich. Is it not a fact that
foreigners from Central Europe have been going into Canada
in the proportion of two to one as compared with British
immigrants, and that many foreigners are going into Australia
from the same source, whilst British migrants are coming
back ?

Sir JOHN WARDLAW MILNE : I do not know whether the
question is addressed to me, but the questioner is perfectly
correct in those statements, speaking generally. During the last
few days we have seen figures of the large influx of Italians into

Australia, male and female. I am not saying that that is harmful.

Sir HENRY LAWRENCE[1]: When not being a member of this Society I received the honour of an invitation to address it, I studied a speech which Sir John delivered in the Guildhall last month. This dealt with emigration within the Empire ; and I would like to say a few words on this point. I agree with a later speaker, Dr. Bentwich, that the circulation of men is more important than even the circulation of money.

Too often in recent years the interests of money have been preferred to the interests of Man ; and the present chaos in the world is in large measure due to the efforts of man to re-establish his mastery over money. That was the keynote of Sir John's previous address, and his able analysis of Currency and Trade movements illustrates the same conclusion to-day.

I come now to Dr. Bentwich. The nations are on the march, as in other great epochs of history. How can we guide and direct the march ?

It has been recognised in countless discussions of the problems of the British Empire that the vast empty spaces must be filled up ; but no one knows how this can be done.

Dr. Bentwich calls attention to the success of the migrations recently effected by the Zionist movement, and I suggest that their methods deserve the study of the numerous bodies that foster emigration, and not least of the Government.

The first obstacle is the insistence of existing populations on the restriction of immigration. Let us take Australia as an example.

Our Australian cousins do not look ahead any further than the average Englishman. Has the conflict between China and Japan impressed their minds with the land-hunger that affects the over-populated countries of the world ? And can they still cling to the hope that a population of seven millions will be left in peaceful possession of an area of three million square miles ? Is not the devastation of Shanghai and Nanking a warning to the citizens of Melbourne and Sydney ?

---

[1] Owing to lack of time at the end of the Session, Sir Henry Lawrence was unable to make orally the comments that here follow. They are, however, printed as a direct contribution to the debate.

But we shall be told that the financial difficulties of large-scale immigration are insuperable. So we were told in regard to the financing of the Great War. When driven by the spur of necessity, the financial experts of every country devised methods which were formerly declared to be impossible. Under sufficient compulsion they will devise a practicable scheme for emigration also, and that is why the Jewish persecutions may serve for our enlightenment.

The transportation from Germany, Poland and Russia in the last few years of tens of thousands of poverty-stricken Jews (and many of them from city slums) has been a wonderful achievement ; and the recent Royal Commission on Palestine has noted with admiration their success in transforming barren wastes and malarial swamps into fertile fields and orchards.

The method of advancing loans to emigrants is no doubt attended with risks. The ample securities demanded by British banks must be foregone ; but if the Jews, whom we may recognise as the past-masters of credit in all the ages, have discovered a way to solve this intractable problem, let our Government and our British leaders of finance be not too proud to learn the secrets of their success.

These obstacles were truly formidable ; the selection of men and women suitable for agricultural life overseas ; their transport, settlement on the land, maintenance till their crops or stock had given them economic stability ; but all these obstacles have been overcome in the past by private enterprise ; and are being overcome to-day by the Zionist organisations.

Is it possible to link up this question of our own emigration with the Peace of Europe ? What would be the result of an invitation to Continental nations to co-operate in a scheme for peopling these empty spaces ? If we examine the history in the last century of the immigration from Central and Southern Europe into Canada and the United States, can we deny that the road is easier now than then ? There are large tracts there in which the common speech is a Continental language ; and these people had organised their own transport, the purchase of their homesteads, and their own maintenance till the lands became productive. They triumphed over incredible hardships without any help from their Government or powerful Associations.

Never was there such enthusiasm to escape from the tyrannies and war-fevers of Europe as there is now ; and never was there a better chance of utilising the advantages which we possees for the relief of humanity in the peace and freedom of the Commonwealth.

These are not the terms which will commend this scheme to the totalitarian Governments elsewhere ; and the negotiations to secure their agreement will not be easy.

In the House of Lords, Lord Samuel discussed the point in regard to Germany, and observed : " So long as Britain had command of the seas, the outlying colonial possessions of other Powers were not necessarily military assets to them. They might rather be pledges of tranquillity."

This was indeed the argument that weighed with Prince Bismarck when for long years he opposed the German Colonial Party in their demand for annexations. It is on record that he wished that the areas abroad where Germans established economic enterprises should not be integral parts of the German Empire, but that the German subjects should be protected against foreign aggression. He advocated autonomous powers of administration by the firms concerned.

It will be objected that the day of chartered companies is past and gone. True, but there are other modes of accommodation open to patient diplomacy.

With good will the most incongruous systems can work side by side in peace and amity. Look at the Indian Federation now coming to birth. What astonishing abnormalities that covers ! e.g., in the union in one constitution of the autocracies of Indian Princes and the democracies of British provinces. We find in Africa a similar distinction between regions under the direct rule of British officers and under the indirect rule of numerous Kings, Sultans and Chiefs—Potentates who are sometimes as irresponsible as European dictators.

In another sphere we see the adherents of Social Credit at work, and the financial experiments of Mr. Aberhart in Canada.

The truth is that the Commonwealth has a broad shield and that there is tolerance for all men who seek to advance the welfare of man; and, as Mr. Chamberlain observed at Edinburgh, the welfare of their own people is also the objective of Modern Dictators.

Let me conclude with the submission that the British Commonwealth is the ideal League of Nations in a practical working model. The only difference between the two is that the League does not work and the Commonwealth does.

Sir ARCHIBALD WEIGALL : I have no doubt that many of you present were here on the opening day, and will be here to-morrow, and that you will say, " This is all very splendid. We have had interesting discussions from eminently qualified men, but where does it all lead to ? Because if we are simply going to sit down and chew the cud, obviously the object of this Conference will have been lost. Let me make it quite clear that this Conference was designed to cover the whole world problem. We began with the relation of the Dominions to the British Empire. We went on at the third Session with one of the most remarkable addresses I have ever heard on the relation of the Colonial Empire, that by Lord Dufferin, and now we have come to the world problem. To-morrow we end up with Production versus Consumption. That has been done designedly. The Press have been excluded designedly, and by arrangement with the Secretary of State for the Dominions and Colonies, it will be my job with my advisers here, to give the Government a summary of these discussions. Furthermore, in the case of the British Broadcasting Corporation, I am to be allowed to make a long broadcast to the whole of the Empire on the Empire wavelength on December 6th.[1]

I agree with what Sir Alan Anderson and Sir Patrick Hannon have said. During the last six years I have devoted my life entirely to this Society, and one of my first reactions has been tremendous gratitude for having the opportunity to discuss with everybody who really counts as a leader of thought and action within the Empire, and particularly this year, with other leaders who came to the Coronation and did us the honour of coming here to discuss affairs in an unofficial atmosphere.

I am convinced that everybody in the Empire desires to lead an ordered economic life in an atmosphere of international peace, but I am also convinced that the Empire as a whole is not united in thought as to how that is to be achieved, and our job, and the big job that we can do at this Conference, is to try

---

[1] This broadcast was actually delivered on the appointed day.

and unite Imperial thought all over the Empire on this great problem.

I am sure Sir Alan Anderson will agree with me that there is one, if not more, of our Dominions who would share more nearly the view expressed by Sir Patrick Hannon. As long as human nature is what it is, the obvious immediate reaction of a Dominion Government is " How is this going to affect our people, irrespective of the British Empire as a whole, and irrespective of the world problem ? "

Mr. McDougall in his excellent address at the first Session, made it quite clear that while he hitched his waggon to a very high star, he realised the enormous difficulties of uniting the thought of Dominions Governments all over the Empire to attain these very desirable ends, and therefore, while keeping our ideals as high as possible, I realise the enormous difficulty. It is dreadful, but true to reflect that there is not in a single University to-day a Chair of Imperial Relations. There are Chairs of History dealing with the past, but not a single Chair from which the Professor is trying to inculcate the sort of view that we have heard expressed here.

Here in the Royal Empire Society we have a home for Imperial Relations, where there is some unity of thought and action. In addition we have an incomparable library and a newspaper room where there can be found the last issue of every important newspaper published within the British Empire. Are we going to make a real use of it ?

I frankly confess that this Conference was designed to try to give a push to the establishment of that sort of fundamental engine for getting unity of thought throughout the British Empire on these world problems. The time is more than ripe, and if this Conference does nothing else, it will satisfy the hopes of all of those who have so splendidly supported us in opening up an entirely new avenue of thought and action. We have always in the past been looked upon to a large extent as the old die-hard, ex pro-consul type who sits back and says, " By gad, Sir, when we were on the frontier. . . . " We have to get a new atmosphere. I rose to point out that we have all this in mind and we hope as a result of your kindly interest in our first efforts, to be able to make a real contribution to the problems so admirably put before us.

Lady ELEANOR COLE : I feel nervous in rising before such an audience of experts, but I am speaking as a producer of a raw material. I produce wool in East Africa, and as such I have been greatly concerned at seeing a country like Germany, that in the past has been a big user of wool, trying to produce it synthetically. In consequence I have deep sympathy for the point of view expressed by various speakers of the danger of this ultranationalist policy—each nation aiming at being self-supporting.

Other speakers have asked that we might be not merely negative in our policy, and I should like to ask Sir John if he could outline to us what the alternative is to that self-supporting policy ? It seems to me that the alternative must be to encourage each nation to produce that for which each is best suited. Are we not also a little to blame in tending towards this national self-sufficiency ? For instance, I caught myself to-day looking in a toy shop, and instinctively turning away from toys marked as foreign. But are we supreme as toy makers ? Are not other countries rather better ? If it is not to be our policy to be wholly self-supporting, ought we not all to be encouraged to buy such goods as other countries make better than we do ? I do not want to take the bread from the toy makers of this country, but if we were encouraged to buy foreign-made toys might it not result in those toy-making countries being able to spend more money in this country on, say, Bradford cloth and so in the end mean just as much employment here and better trade all round ?

Mr. THOMAS DUNBABIN[1]: I am here to reassure Sir Patrick Hannon. I think he need have no apprehension about this American trade treaty unless something is done greatly exceeding the rate at which things have moved so far. The treaty was first suggested two years ago. We have now got to the stage when it is expected that we shall shortly exchange lists. For many years people have protested against the treaty, and it seems to me that unless the political aspect overwhelms the economic, the Trade Treaty will either not be made, or will be so harmless that no one need worry.

The real difficulty is that unless someone gives away some-

---

[1] DUNBABIN, Thomas, M.A. (University of Tasmania). Editor of the *Sun*, Sydney, New South Wales. Editor and Manager, Australian Newspaper Cable Service. Rhodes Scholar for Tasmania, 1906–9.

thing, the Treaty might just as well not be made. Is it better to give something to our friends—assuming that Americans are our friends—in return for a certain amount of political security, or be forced to give something to people who are our potential enemies ? Apart from this the relation of different parts of the Empire with each other and the world needs revision. Sir Alan Anderson and Mr. McDougall think it is time we made the British Empire a reality, which I believe can be done.

What is the British Empire ? That is a question for Sir Archibald Weigall. It is the greatest conception the world has yet known, and it is in danger of falling into a slough of small considerations, as to whether we shall sell five shillings worth of butter here or there. I prefer the picture of the speaker who showed us Great Britain and the Empire facing Germany with a pat of butter in one hand and a gun in the other, saying, " Take which you will ". That is a reasonable attitude and I am all in favour of it, and if you point the gun straight enough and they believe it is loaded, they will take the butter. We saw that clearly when British diplomacy sat up straight and spoke straight to the Italians. They said, " Yes, Mr. Eden, thank you very much. We should like to come in and stop the submarine policy. We have had nothing to do with it, but there won't be any more." And there has not been.

Let us face the facts. The British Empire is a cumbersome, awkward machine. In this question of trade treaties, first we consult with America, then with the Dominions, then with the Colonies, going round and round, and unless we are careful, the circle will never be completed. There is nobody to speak for the Empire. The Royal Empire Society might do it, if it were given authority. If I want to make a trade treaty with Berlin, I go to Berlin and make my treaty. If I want a treaty with the United States I go to Washington, but as the result of the Ottawa Agreements if we want to make a trade treaty we have to go to London, South Africa, Capetown, Ottawa, Canberra, and Wellington in New Zealand. It is a dreadful truth, and when we come to our foreign policy the position is worse. I do not think the Germans or Italians know what our foreign policy is, and they wonder if we have one at all. We have to think very hard about the Empire. Conferences are admirable, but

K

it is also necessary to think hard. It is no good being too confident and too satisfied that everything is going well, and that Mr. Chamberlain and Mr. Mackenzie King are settling the affairs of the world. We must think for ourselves and then we shall be able to make the Empire a success.

REPLY

Sir JOHN WARDLAW-MILNE : My reply will be extremely short for two reasons. In the first place the time is limited, and secondly to some extent, as always happens, speakers have answered each other. Differing views, however, have been expressed on one or two matters which I referred to. I want to take up the point made by the Chairman, with which I agree, that the problem which I had the privilege of putting before you is not entirely economic. I stressed that point also, but did not go into details on the political problem, because it would be impossible to do so in one address. It would be extremely difficult to do it justice in any case as we might all hold different views as to the correct solution in different parts of the world. I do not hesitate to repeat, however, what I said before, and I do not think you will disagree, that difficult and important as is the political aspect, the world problem is fundamentally economic and not political. It is self-sufficiency and nationalism, of which I spoke, which are hindering world development and prosperity and this again is, in itself, an economic problem. The movement really arises from poverty. A large number of these nations have not the money or the means to trade, and this movement for self-sufficiency will not be reversed unless a means can be provided to bring these peoples back to the full extent to which their population entitles them in world trade. It is that aspect of the matter which I specially tried to emphasise to you to-day. Let me put forward in that connection again the suggestion that the advancement that has been made in securing the exchange of goods between nations can perhaps be developed still more by a further lead from this country.

I wish to dissent a little from the views of the last speaker (Mr. Dunbabin) in connection with his remarks as to the lead which the Empire has given.

This country and the Empire, in the setting up of a currency policy for the sterling area and by agreement with France and the United States, has done a great deal to help world trade. The great problem is to extend these arrangements in such a way as to secure that those nations with no facilities for trading at present will be able to come into the circle. The problem is largely a problem of poverty of certain nations : poverty breeds fear, and fear breeds war. We must break down isolation, and that can only be done by political action in the first instance. In the end, however, it is a problem of curing the economic ills of the world.

I am sure you will not expect me to go into the details of the possible development of a tariff policy which would embrace the world. I do not know what form world negotiations will take. They may take the form of lower or higher tariffs, with various changes due to very varying conditions. I am convinced that the world problem is essentially an economic one.

V

THE RELATION BETWEEN PRODUCTION AND CONSUMPTION

Thursday, November 25th.   Fifth Session

Mr. C. G. AMMON[1] in the Chair : I am glad to have the opportunity of presiding over this important Conference on a subject of vital importance to us all. I have the privilege of introducing a distinguished Professor of Economics, which reminds me that there are several descriptions of economists, one being that they are rather like Christopher Columbus who when he set out didn't know where he was going : when he got there, did not know where he was, and when he came back, could not say where he had been ! Our particular economist is a good deal in advance of that class. He is going to tell us where we are going, and many of us would be grateful to know where we are.   Professor Hall[2] is one of a distinguished school of younger economists : he has courage, for he has actually written a book on that mysterious subject, ' The Exchange Equalisation Fund '.   Personally I have never met anyone who understood the subject !

That should be enough to introduce our Professor, who will talk on the relation between Production and Consumption. That is an important subject at the present time when we are faced with the appalling fact that never was productive capacity at such a height as it is at present, and yet we are faced with the extraordinary problem that about one-half of the world's population is on the verge of starvation. How those two facts are to be related we shall be glad to hear from Professor Noel Hall.

[1] AMMON, Charles George, J.P. M.P. (Labour) for North Camberwell, 1922–31. Parliamentary Secretary to the Admiralty, 1924 and 1929–31. Member of London County Council, 1919–25 and since 1934.
[2] HALL, Noel Frederick, M.A. Professor of Political Economy in the University of London. Commonwealth Fund Fellow in Economics, Princeton University, U.S.A., 1925–27. Secretary of Fellowship Advisory Committee of Rockefeller Foundation for Social Sciences in Great Britain and Ireland.

Professor N. F. HALL: When I received the invitation of your Committee to address you to-day, I was preparing to leave Sydney and to travel by land across the Commonwealth of Australia in order to complete a trip round the world. With a small matter of a journey of say 14,000 miles in front and the exhilarating experience of four months in Sydney behind me, I felt that I could take on anything, singe the King of Spain's beard, put my telescope to my blind eye, and do all those other heroic things that are possible in imagination. To discuss the relationship between consumption and production seemed only another step in a gay adventure. But to-day, far removed from the Sydney sun and at the start of my third successive winter and asked to follow the galaxy of talent and experience which has already addressed you, I must admit that the gunpowder is running out of the heels of my boots. I can now sympathise with the candidates for high honours in the old days in the Chinese Universities who had to face an examination which consisted of one question only: " Write down all you know ". Because in effect that is what you have asked me to do.

Economics is really the study of the relationship between consumption and production, and it is only worth studying when that is steadily born in mind. The word itself recalls to us the old Greek household over which the head of the family, the true patriot king, presided, guided by the wise rules of household management in his high duty of providing for the well-being of all those entrusted to his care. He found in their welfare the justification of all his policies, and the eighteenth century was wiser than it knew when it took the words $\delta\iota\kappa\iota\alpha$ $\nu o\mu os$ to replace the more clumsy title " Political Arithmetic " under which economic studies had previously been carried on.

But in the modern world the chain of events that link together consumption and production is so complex that a real effort of the imagination and a disciplined control of the mind is necessary in scrutinising our economic policies and our production activities. There has long been a tendency to regard 'production' as in some special sense its own justification, particularly when it involves the creation of new and exciting products or the use of complex and mysterious technological processes. No less a person than Adam Smith himself dropped into this, the easiest of economic fallacies. He denied to anyone whose efforts did not result in some tangible product the title of ' Productive Labourer', and he built up his theory of the wealth of nations upon the doctrine that the welfare of a people depends upon the proportion that the ' productive ' bear to the ' unproductive ' labourers. He would, on this account, have given to many of us at this Conference short shrift. Let me quote the remarkable passage in which he disposes by implication of myself, and also, I fear, of nearly all those who are taking part as Speakers or Chairmen, and many of the listeners, at this Conference :

". . . The labour of some of the most respectable orders in the society is, like that of menial servants, unproductive of any value, and does not fix or realise itself in any permanent subject, or vendible commodity, which endures after that labour is past, and for which an equal quantity of labour could afterwards be procured. The sovereign, for example, with all the officers both of justice and war who serve under him, the whole Army and Navy, are unproductive labourers. . . . In the same class must be ranked, some both of the gravest and most important, some of the most frivolous professions, churchmen, lawyers, physicians, men of letters of all kinds ; players, buffoons, musicians, opera-singers, opera-dancers, etc. The labour of the meanest of these has a certain value, regulated by the very same principles which regulate that of every other sort of labour ; and that of the noblest and most useful, produces nothing which could afterwards purchase or procure an equal quantity of labour. Like the declamation of the actor, the harangue of the orator, or the tune of the musician, the work of all of them perishes in the very instant of its production. . . ."

I think this passage is an admirable illustration of the dangerous mental twists that men can indulge in when they concentrate too much upon production and do not consider production in relation to consumption. If Adam Smith is taken seriously, his own great principle of the advantages of the division of labour disappears and society can become wealthy only by the process of heedless increases in its physical output. This is demonstrably not the case.

It is, therefore, valuable to approach the problem of economic progress and development from the other end and to ask in what way consumption is likely to increase and to change in a progressive society. It is only by asking this question that we get any reasonable basis upon which to plan our economic development. Economic progress nearly always takes the form of diversifying consumption, by adding butter to bread, and then jam to the bread and butter, and so on and on steadily diversifying and changing the sort of things that are consumed as people get 'better-off'. When we talk about increasing consumption, we very rarely mean equal proportional increases in the supplies of all the goods now being consumed. What is usually wanted is a big increase in certain types of goods and a relatively small increase in other types. Over the last hundred years there has clearly been in England a big increase in the meat consumption per head of the population. There has been a very much smaller increase in the bread consumption per head. Progress has also involved the introduction of entirely new goods ; bicycles, gramophones, wireless sets, motor-cars, cinemas, electric light, and countless other things which had no place in the economy of one hundred years ago. The coming of these things served a double purpose. It has increased the opportunities for earning income on the part of those who produced the new goods, with the result that money earnings all round have been raised. This addition to the net earnings of the economy has sustained and increased the demand for the old types of goods and has made economically possible improvements in methods of production generally, with further consequential improvements in the standard of life of all. Neither step would have been effective without the other ; it has been the harmonious adjustment of costs and earnings in the production of goods both new and old which has made the permanent and continuing improvement in consumption possible. The basic principle of economic progress and one that is well fortified by historical experiences drawn from past eras which have been characterised by increasing scientific knowledge, is that improvements in consumption must be associated with diversification of output.

If, therefore, we are to plan the economic development of the Empire upon a sound basis, we have to make sure that the tendency for consumption to change as income rises is not frustrated by the incapacity of production to adapt itself to the new needs and wishes of consumers. In broad terms, the

problem of economic progress and development is the problem
of maintaining a flexible production system. Anything that
tends to become unduly rigid and to prevent the making of new
goods in new ways or to check the release of purchasing power
for new goods by changes in the methods, and in particular
by reductions in the costs of making old goods must tend to
delay and retard progress.

If, therefore, we are to discuss the problem of Empire development, we must try to see if it is possible to indicate in broad outline the main direction in which consumption is likely to change
during the next fifteen or twenty years. If we can do that, we
have some guide which we can use to check our measures of
practical policy, which should be designed to retard certain lines
of production and to stimulate others.

If we look back over the changes in consumption in England
over the past thirty years, we can see now that there are some
things which we ought reasonably to have been able to foresee
even in 1907, and other things that we could not have foreseen.
We could not have foreseen all those rapid improvements in
technical knowledge which made possible the cheap motor-car
and the problem of the roads, the rapid development of the
cinema, the possibility of mass production, of electrical energy
at very low prices. Nor could we have foreseen the world war
and the totality of its effect upon economic and social life, and
also upon the rate and character of the development of technological knowledge. But assuming that we had resolved in 1907
that our economic progress should take the form of improved
consumption, that is of a better standard of life in this country,
there would, I think, have been certain changes that we could
have foreseen. We should have been looking forward to the
disappearance from our streets of the ragged children with no
shoes and stockings, we should have been looking forward to the
disappearance of the worst slum conditions; we should have
been able to detect the general direction in which people would
have to increase their consumption of meat, milk, butter and
fruit in order to obtain under the climatic conditions of our
country a better standard of living.

Is our position in 1937 very greatly different from that which
we might have imagined in 1907? We have to face the situations
where, if we cut out political uncertainties, we know that techni-

cal progress is developing very rapidly. There are waiting round
the corner a large variety of new products which will create new
opportunities for employment and new industrial activity both
in this country and throughout the Empire, which will give a
powerful stimulus to the earning capacity of the Empire as a
whole. We cannot predict in detail exactly what these changes
in productive capacity are likely to be, but I think we do already
know enough to be able to indicate now the probable direction
in which there will be improvements in consumption.

Sir John Boyd Orr has carried out a detailed study of the
quantities of different types of foodstuffs which are consumed
at different levels of income in this country. Sir John Orr's
enquiry enables us to indicate the particular directions in which
increases in consumption are particularly desirable if the standard of the lower income groups is to be raised, to the minimum
necessary for nutritionally 'perfect' health. While the data upon
which this enquiry was based were meagre in quantity and not
strictly representative in quality so that the margin of error in
the final figures which emerges from it may be large, nevertheless, the results are in harmony with information obtained in
other ways and with historical experience of the general trend
of changes in dietary. We can, therefore, accept the results of
the investigation as giving in broad outline a guide to the existing deficiencies in diets in this country during the present decade.
To make up the deficiencies and to secure that national dietary
which is necessary for ' perfect ' health, the total consumption
of the different kinds of foodstuffs will have to be increased by
approximately the following percentages :

Butter	.	.	. 20 per cent
Milk .	.	.	. 16 ,,
Eggs .	.	.	. 15 ,,
Fruits	.	.	. 25 ,,
Vegetables	.	.	. 25 ,,
Meat .	.	.	. 12 ,,

and in the light of nutritional knowledge when the survey was
taken there ought to be some reduction in the per capita consumption of margarine.

Turn these percentages into physical quantities and the
results are startling. Approximately 800 million gallons of milk
are needed, 2 million hundredweight of butter, 15 million great

hundreds of eggs, 8 million hundredweight of meat, and assuming that the present proportions of different types of fruit remain constant, we require an additional 4 million hundredweights of apples, 3 million more bunches of bananas, 6 million hundredweights of other fruits, and 8 million hundredweights of vegetables other than potatoes.

It is difficult to grasp figures of this order of magnitude, or to see what they mean, unless there is something with which to compare them. I propose to compare them with the figures for the increased imports into Britain over the twenty-five years, 1909–34. In meat the needed increase in total supplies is more than the total increase in the British imports in the period, 1909–34. In eggs the total increase in supplies is larger than the increase in imports; in apples the needed increase is double the increase in imports, and what is true of apples is true of all the other fruits. In butter we need an increase in supplies equal to one and a half times the total British imports. In milk there should be a substantial increase in total output.

I have used the figures of the increase in imports simply as a basis for comparison. I am not arguing that we can or should obtain all the increased supplies which we need from imports. On the contrary, I am sure that the right way to secure Sir John Orr's objective is to re-think relationships between our home production and our overseas purchases of foodstuffs of all types. I have used the figures of the increase of imports between 1909– 34 solely to serve as an indicator of the scale upon which progress has got to be made before we can be content with our economic achievements. Viewed from the consumption end, the scope for urgently needed economic development is plain. We must not allow the quite exceptional difficulties of the post-War period, 1921–29, and the events of the subsequent world depression to blind us to the extent of our opportunities. Nor is there anything particularly new or strange in the task that lies ahead. It is one in which we already have over a century of experience. The improvements of dietaries as the standard of life has been raised has been continuing ever since the Industrial Revolution. During the past twenty years a great deal of public interest has been focussed upon general or average prices, what is usually loosely called the 'price level', and the much more important subject of *relative* prices has been lost sight of.

This has been only natural in a period dominated by the special financial and monetary disturbances induced by the necessities of war-time borrowing and post-War funding. While no one can favour large scale variations in prices of the kind which took place during and after the War and again during 1929–32, it is necessary if there is to be both improved production and more beneficial consumption that we should reconcile ourselves to the vital necessity for changes in relative prices and particularly in the retail prices of those goods in which there are marked deficiencies in consumption.

Such goods being protective rather than energy-giving foods are particularly sensitive to price changes and can easily be displaced from the dietaries of the mass of the people not only by a rise in their own prices, but equally as the result of increases in the prices of other more essential foodstuffs. To keep down the cost of the basic necessaries of life to the lowest possible point and to keep down the costs of distributing and retailing them is the surest possible way of releasing and stimulating demand for quality goods. And the production and handling of such additional protective foods will require considerable development in industrial production, the organisation of transport of all kinds, storage devices, home equipment and the like.

There is indeed a sufficient volume of latent economic enterprise lying behind the consumption programme which I have broadly outlined to guarantee a period of active trade for the United Kingdom for the next generation. The opportunity is great despite the fact that we have to look forward to a decline in population.

It is, therefore, essential that the policy in the home market should be as closely linked as possible with our consumption programme for raising the standard of living. To try and to keep up the price of milk for human consumption in order to keep down the price of milk for manufacture in order to recapture a lost export trade for powdered milk—a point which was solemnly argued before an official Committee of Enquiry not very long ago—is short-sighted to the extreme. It tends to arrest that development in consumption which should be the basis of further economic development and progress in the United Kingdom as a whole.

Recent studies in changes in consumption during the past century in dietaries in this and in other countries confirm the main trend of the conclusions reached by Sir John Orr's investigation. Even before exact knowledge of nutritional requirements was available, the instinctive needs of the people caused them to shift and to diversify their consumption very much along the lines which recent scientific knowledge has indicated that it should be increased and diversified in the future. I think, therefore, that we can safely rely as a guide for future policy upon any general consumption programme that is built upon Sir John Orr's analysis, and the events of the subsequent world depression to blind us to the extent of our opportunities. Nor is there anything particularly new or strange in the task that lies ahead. It is one in which we already have over a century of experience. The improvement of dietaries as the standard of life has varied has been continuing ever since the maligned industrial revolution, and there for the moment I must leave the consumption programme for the United Kingdom.

Meanwhile I want to swing right away from Great Britain to the tropical Colonial Empire, and more particularly to the African Colonies. Here we find exactly the same problem in a much more complex form. It is impossible to draw up a programme of desirable consumption giving the net additional quantities of foodstuffs of different types which are needed to give reasonable nutritional standard to the native population. The data are not available. But that enormous opportunities for improving consumption lie ahead is sufficiently indicated by a series of examples drawn from different sources, either of official reports publicly issued by some of the Colonial Governments, or by studies prepared by anthropologists and other field investigators. The mass of material is so large that it is difficult to select from it.

There are, however, certain points in common throughout the whole. There is a close relationship between the incidence of certain types of disease and certain marked deficiencies in dietaries. In some cases it is the problem of shortage of milk and meat, in others it is the shortage of karotine or of certain types of mineral salts. But in all cases difficulties arise because of the extremely small scale upon which the economic life of the native population is at present carried on, and because of the difficulties of making changes in social and economic practices which persist.

Here, for example, is a report published by the Government of Uganda, upon An Investigation into Health and Agriculture in Teso, Uganda. For the purpose of this study two different tribal groups living under somewhat similar conditions were compared, and the report concludes as follows :—

". . . The first, and most obvious observation is that nutritional disease is more prevalent in Ajuluku than in Opami, and that it might be possible to improve dietary and agricultural conditions in Ajuluku by imitating the conditions obtained in Opami. The comparison of significance between correlation co-efficients in Ajuluku and Opami suggests that fish in the diet is one of the main causes of superior health (probably referable mainly to the absence of ulcer) in the latter area. In this connection the reader is referred to the most recent work on this problem at present available, that of Brown (1935) and Clements (1934). The latter investigator, using statistical methods, found that tropical ulcer was confined chiefly to natives who lived on a high carbohydrate, low-protein diet, and that the addition of fish had a most beneficial effect on health in this respect. Hence the addition of animal food seems desirable in the more vegetarian parts of Teso, and probably of other districts.

The only feasible method of procuring this is to encourage the slaughter and consumption of bullocks. There are in Teso at least 60 thousand non-working male cattle after optimum ploughing requirements have been fulfilled (allowing 4 oxen to each of the 14 thousand ploughs for between 25 and 30 acres per plough). The great difficulty which will be encountered in introducing this revolutionary project lies in the native's idea that his cattle are his capital (cf. the derivation of the English word 'pecuniary' from pecus, a herd of cattle, Lat.)."

The same sort of conclusion arises from all the other studies. Drs. Burnet and Akroyd, in their report, "Nutrition and Public Health", call attention to the fact that the protein intake of the native populations in the tropics and the East is usually small. The Masai in British East Africa, who live mainly on meat, milk and blood, and whose protein consumption is from 200–300 grammes a day, are exceptional. The bulk of the diet of most of the native population is composed of cereals, but it has been noted that in certain districts an increase in prosperity brings about a rise in the consumption of wheat. " In general ", their Report concludes, " there is a constant insufficiency of meat, milk, grain and vegetables, and a certain lack of animal fats, and in many parts of Africa there are deficiencies in sodium chloride, so that salt is a valuable article of merchandise." One of the most important deficiencies of all, because it affects stock raising as well as human consumption, is a general soil deficiency in phosphorus, but this deficiency is not peculiar to Africa; it is common to large parts of the world and can be rectified by artificial means.

The general upshot of all studies is the same. The demands made upon the medical and administrative services in the discharge of the duties of colonial trusteeship are high largely because nutritional standards are low. There lies before us a great opportunity for the practice of the only sound form of economy, that of deviating expenditure now incurred for curative and remedial purposes to attack the root causes of the difficulties of the native populations, that is the inadequacy and lack of diversification in their customary dietaries.

The results of the present condition are a large variety of diseases ; night blindness, pellagra, tropical ulcer and the like, all of which result from either badly balanced or deficient dietaries. And on top of the whole problem is the fundamental one of 'unemployment of resources'. In the United Kingdom our unemployed resources appear partly as a plethora of cash and partly in the monthly reports of the Ministry of Labour upon the state of the register of the unemployed work-people. In the Colonial Empire we have the increasing problem of soil erosion, which is unemployed or misemployed land, and the unemployed capital, which in the case I have just cited takes the form of sterile and useless oxen which destroy the pastures causing the top soil to be washed into the sea and creates a major problem for the Colonial administration.

An article by H. S. Scott in the recent volume *Africa*, the Journal of the International Institute of African Languages and Cultures, shows how this situation might be met ; the educational Department was called in to help to assist in the difficulties of the administration in a district of Turkana. The local population had lost their cattle owing to the prevalence of cattle disease and Tsetse-fly, and the area, owing to soil erosion, was definitely inhospitable.

". . . The situation seemed a grim one. What could an Education Department do under such circumstances ? The most urgent need appeared to be to provide the tribe with the means of securing a greater variety of crops, so that the risk of failure of one crop might be compensated by the success of others, possibly more resistant to drought. It is perhaps important to emphasise that what struck us at the time was the urgent need for the provision of an increased *quantity* of food ; we ourselves had not the knowledge, nor was technical advice available to enable us even if we had thought of it, to talk about nutritive *values*. When the education authorities had received the report of the officer, they decided with some hesitation to open a school for about forty boys at the head-quarters of the district. The inducement offered to the parents to send their boys to school was that the school was to be a boarding school, so that the pupils would certainly get enough to eat. In education, as generally understood, it was obviously not yet possible to interest the people of the tribe. The purpose of the school from the very beginning was to teach the boys how to grow things suitable for the country in which they lived. Incidentally, of course, the ordinary work of a school was to be carried on, but the prime function was as I have stated. With this end in view, the pupils recruited were of different ages. It was not possible to start with boys all of whom were of tender age. Some boys had to be old enough and strong enough to do the initial clearing for and to help in the cultivation of the large school gardens which were the central feature and main purpose of the school.

The first area to be cleared was a piece of land about $1\frac{1}{2}$ acres in extent. Rough fencing was erected to give as much security as possible from the depredation of game. This was the main school plot in which the pupils were to be taught, and in it, when the rains came in April, there were planted European potatoes, maize, tomatoes, carrots, cabbages, onions and spinach. Early in July the fertile soil of the garden produced a bumper crop, and the first reaction of the boys was one of wonder that on so small a plot so large an amount of produce could be secured. The crop was, of course, entirely strange to them, but when they were given the potatoes to eat as part of the school ration, they found them pleasant and very filling. The boys at once set about clearing and preparing gardens of their own. They had been given permission to have gardens when the school opened, but the real incentive which made them to start work on their own was the bumper crop of appetising food which they had seen produced on the school plot.

It was fortunate that about the time when this crop was reaped there was a meeting of the local native council of the tribe held at the headquarters of the district near the school. Advantage was taken of this opportunity to invite the elders to visit and inspect the school. When they were invited to sample the produce their interest was immediately aroused in the school as a place of practical utility. The local native council came to the conclusion that anything which helped to fill their stomachs was worth encouraging, whatever its name might be ; indeed, if we had asked a Suk then what a school was, he would have said: " A school is a place where you eat potatoes. . . ."

These last words are significant. A school in this district becomes " a place where you eat potatoes ". In other words, in which modern knowledge has been effectively applied to the problem of idle resources and empty stomachs, and there has been an increase in the work because production has been stimulated even under difficult conditions by the superior technical knowledge of the Educational Department. Continuously applied on a larger scale, this method may even get over the difficulty of the surplus oxen which waste the land. A wise eighteenth-century Irish Bishop, probably of the Father O'Flynn type, when he was criticised for concerning himself with mundane things instead of his spiritual tasks, answered his critics, " Is not the creation of wants the best way to make a people industrious ? " Is not this Irish bull the appropriate answer to the surplus African oxen ?

There can be great increases in the productivity of the tropical Empire by making available modern knowledge and by increasing the wants of the people. What will be essential will be cheap means of communication, cheap transport, cheap bicycles and the other equipment necessary to make the people aware of their opportunities and to overcome their local isolations. These things will have to be supplied from overseas and should provide a new dynamic stimulus to international trade generally. The need for them relates the problem of increasing the consumption of the tropical Empire with our own need for improved dietaries in the United Kingdom. The opportunity of achieving both ends can only be realised if there is a recovery in general international trade. But before dealing with this point, I want to look briefly at another and different region of the Empire where a different type of consumption programme is needed for future development.

Australia is now embarking upon a new phase of her development. Resort to new lands is becoming increasingly difficult, and the problem is to increase the productivity both per head and per acre of land already employed. Closer settlement, more intensive methods of cultivation and diversification of crops and of local industry have become the order of the day. Provided that really cheap transport can be provided, there should be a continual tendency to diversification of production and lower unit costs. If this intensification of effort is successful, Australia will need cheaper motor-cars and aeroplanes, more petrol, much cheaper housing materials and considerable capital re-equipment. She will, however, have an even larger surplus of primary products of a variety of types. The day is not far distant when she will also have in some special cases a surplus of industrial products.

Until the present troubles in China started, Australia was finding a steadily expanding outlet for her primary and even her industrial products in the Far East, which has now replaced Europe (excluding the United Kingdom) as Australia's second-best customer. In an attempt to keep her hold upon the English market, Australia recently embroiled herself in a most unfortunate trade dispute with Japan, which resulted in a serious loss of exports with practically no falling off of imports. The result was a loss of the sterling exchange which Australia must have to maintain her financial position and to provide the service for the overseas capital which she needs if her internal developments are to continue.

L

And the importance to Australia of exports and the Far East market brings me to the point of unity in my three separate consumption programmes. Australia must have outlets larger than those which can be found in the United Kingdom if she is to dispose of her exports and to maintain her development and increase her consumption. These outlets she is only likely to find in the industrial world other than the United Kingdom. But these countries cannot buy from Australia and the other Dominions unless they are able to sell, not necessarily to these Dominions direct, but somewhere in an international exchange system.

A number of the newer industrial countries where the need for primary produce is particularly great and which are low quality producers are able to hold their place as industrialist users by using mass production methods and employing relatively unskilled labour. Their products are of the kind and tend to be disposable at prices which make them particularly appropriate to the needs of the poorest peoples living in the tropical world. But these needs cannot be met exclusively by industrial products of this type. Many capital goods of the highest quality will also be needed if economic progress in the colonial Empire is to proceed along such lines. Indeed, there is a close identity of interest between the sellers of the highly finished quality products of the older-established industrial countries and of those who seek to sell the cheaper consumption goods from the newly industrialised countries. The difficulties of Australia with Japan, the needs of the tropical world and the great interest of the United Kingdom in a recovery in the volume of multi-lateral international trade all fit together at this point. If we can introduce a sound development policy in the tropical world, supplying the capital and quality goods ourselves, encouraging others to supply the lower-quality goods and counting upon the supply of such goods to give an economic volume of turnover upon the new capital equipment, we shall stimulate our own trade, reduce direct competition with our exports in other markets, take the pressure off Australia and give a new incentive to the economic life of all parts of the Empire.

The stimulus to the economic progress of the tropical Empire, except in the cases where there is undue dependence upon the export of a single staple product such as sugar, can best be found in the development upon quite a small scale of an export crop of a specialised character in the tropical colonies. The development of such exports will mean that a larger proportion of the population will be producing a cash crop and breaking away from subsistence or traditional production.

The presence in each colony of even a small percentage of men and women who sell their own produce for export and have to be fed out of the surplus of their neighbours will exert a powerful and a far-reaching influence similar to that which links up the feudal system in England and Europe. Money circulates : those who will feed the exporters will in their turn have a surplus of money income to spend. They will tend to buy crops produced in excess of local requirements by other groups and the chain of influence will spread. But these cash crops capable of export are likely to be highly specialised. Coffee, hemp, copra, specialised seeds and oils, and grain, special woods, ores and other raw materials. In quality and value, as the report of the recent League of Nations Committee upon Raw Materials has shown, these exports are likely to be only a very small percentage of world trade. But this is surely a case in which statistics are particularly misleading. I have already tried to show that a relatively small amount of exports may play a large share in stimulating other types of economic activity in the colony concerned. If we look at the matter at the other end, that of the importers, we see that although small in quantity and value, these exports of tropical produce are of great and increasing technical importance to the great industrial countries. It is difficult to devise effective substitutes for them, and if there is to be that big increase in British consumption which I have outlined as desirable, there must be considerable technical improvements in industrial processes here, and in each case technical improvements will probably frequently require some small —probably quite small—increase in the use of specialised tropical produce.

But what is true of the probable trend of industrial progress in the United Kingdom is true also of likely developments in the U.S.A. and in Industrial Europe. No single industrial country is likely to want enough of the specialised exportable products of the tropical Empire to make possible any substantial rate of progress. But taking the industrial world as a whole, we can safely anticipate, unless there is political calamity, a steady increase in the total demand for these products and a demand sufficient to stimulate the general economic life of the tropical Empire as a whole. Thus in the same way as the future of Australia is specially linked up with the Far East and that of Canada with the U.S.A., so is the future of the tropical Colonial Empire and its capacity to consume linked up with the increasing productivity of the industrial world as a whole. We shall not gather the fruits of the services of the devoted band of adminstrators, doctors, scientists, agriculturists, and others who are working under such difficult conditions to improve the standard of living in the tropical Empire until we can widen the scope of their trade with the whole industrial world. My link, then, between desirable and obtainable consumption and production is a great widening of the area of trade. Trade internal to the Empire cannot secure an increase in the productivity of the several parts of the Empire upon a scale wide enough to guarantee the increases in consumption which are necessary to raise the standard of living. We maintained in the British market and in the Colonial Empire, down to 1931–2, an openness of door which was designed to secure a maximum rate of growth. We abandoned that policy partly under the pressure of necessity and partly to put ourselves into a better bargaining position to secure a more progressive policy on the part of other industrial countries and of other Colonial powers. To that extent we are now in a more favourable position to make concessions in return for concessions to us.

But we are face to face with this fundamental difficulty. In negotiating such agreements, there is an inevitable tendency to look backwards and not forwards—to see what we have been doing in the past, and to try and secure that type of production in the future. At a time of crisis and in the middle of an exceptionally severe depression, the aftermath of sweeping changes by a world-wide war, that is probably an acceptable method of procedure. But it is a procedure which will inevitably stabilise both production and consumption if it is carried to excess or retained too long. It is true that we still sit the Lord Chancellor, the Keeper of the King's Conscience, the King's Remembrancer, upon a Woolsack, but it would have been a sorry thing for England and for the Empire if he had reminded the King of nothing but wool, and if England had remained as she was early in the reign of Henry VII, dependent pricipally on exports of wool. The growth of Imperial responsibilities compelled us to look forward instead of back, obliged us to be willing to make changes in order to secure progress. The Empire needs again the same outlook to-day ; it needs to adopt consumption programmes of the kind which I have indicated and to use them as a touch-stone for policy. It will do this not blindly, but reasonably. It is no use pulling down all existing production in the blind hope that new methods will spring up, but it is possible to keep on changing production to secure a larger income and a better diversified consumption. It has been happening all around us during the past twenty years. All the technical questions of exports of capital, monetary standards, tariffs, quotas, subsidies, fall into focus and can be reconciled with one another only in the light of their bearing upon future development, that is, upon increases in consumption. It is, therefore, only for this purpose, increases in consumption, that it is safe to use the complex system of control and regulation which we have built upon in the past years.

Speaking in Sydney on the morrow of the Coronation, I asked what we would like to be the achievement of our free Commonwealth during the reign of his present Majesty, what heritage we would like to leave to usher in what may be a second Elizabethan era. I found my answer in terms of the daily lives of individuals. The people in Britain enjoying a better level of health as the result of improved dietaries, the scourge of disease largely removed for people in the tropical Empire, the loneliness and isolation of Australia lifted by easier and freer inter-communications. I claimed that the realisation of this goal was in no wise more impossible than to have supposed at the Coronation of King George V that we in Sydney would have been able to hear his successor taking the Oath to defend the Empire. The link between our present possibilities and that future goal is to widen and to diversify trade, to secure the co-operation of the Empire as a whole with the world as a whole, to study our production policies in the light of our consumption objectives, to get away from fears of the recent past to a belief in our own future. Our free society is facing an acute crisis. It is on trial for its life in the presence of new and insidious forces of tyranny. Apart from the horrible recourse to war, there is only one answer that it can make to the dictators. We can demonstrate that our democracies are more efficient forms of government than the autocracies; we can challenge a judgment with reference to what in the last resort is the only abiding test of the value of any form of government and that is by the quality of the daily lives of the masses of the people.

The discussion was opened by :

Sir MONTAGUE BARLOW[1]: After the most admirable and well-seasoned philosophical discourse to which we have just listened, I feel myself ill-equipped to follow Professor Hall. We are living in difficult times : that is a commonplace, but unfortunately it is true, and I should like, if Professor Hall will allow me, to put what I have to say in the form of one or two questions to him about these difficulties.

General Smuts used a pregnant phrase recently when he said, " Humanity is again on the march " : he was enlarging on the enormous and rapid changes which as the result both of the war and of recent scientific discoveries ; the aeroplane, wireless, etc., are causing the world to shrink in size almost to that of a parish. And these enormous changes are taking place at a speed which makes the problems involved infinitely more difficult and urgent than a century ago.

Professor Hall has talked to us in the calm atmosphere of the lecture-room. I always admire such assuredness : it straightens out difficulties with so much ease. Omniscience we expect in the lecture room : I only wish we might rely on omnipotence as well. I, like a good many other people in this room, have devoted the larger portion of our lives to administration, to public affairs, whether at home or abroad. Some of us have been busy as administrators, as statesmen, if you please, to find practical solutions to some of the difficulties which the modern world presents : and it is from the practical and administrative point of view that I want to ask one or two questions—in the atmosphere of the lecture room it is not difficult to talk, as he

[1] BARLOW, Rt. Hon. Sir Montague, K.B.E. M.P. (Conservative) for South Salford, 1910–23. Minister of Labour, 1922–4. Senior Government Representative at various International Labour Conferences. Chairman of Royal Commission on the Distribution of Industry.

talks, of ' canalising ' Japanese surplus production. I should like to see Professor Hall face to face with some of my Japanese friends, trying to solve such a problem in a practical way : they would smile agreeably, but I venture to say that at the end of the discussion not very much progress would have been made.

The first question I should like to put is this. Professor Hall mentioned the problem of readjusting production, and I would like to ask him what his attitude is towards what I should like to call reasonable restriction of production ? Please do not misunderstand me. I am not defending restriction in the old sense, when the wicked capitalist was supposed to try and secure a monopoly in order to put up prices. The modern form of restriction is quite different. It is along the lines of trying to balance periods of high flow production to level out the peaks and the depths of great and small production, with a view to securing stability of price and therefore a better economic situation in the market both for producers and for the consumer ; whatever may be said about the blessings of the old happy days of *laissez-faire*, this clearly is obvious, that alternative periods of low production and high prices, and high production and low prices, with all the disorganisation that follows were not satisfactory either to consumer or producer, and the world is tending slowly to move away from it. I need not give examples, but in the world of metals, tin has now become largely a regulated commodity with the object of securing a certain stability of price : and to some extent at any rate, the heights and depths of tin prices have been evened out.

I was presiding recently over a Royal Commission in Canada with regard to the production of coal, and encountered a similar problem there : few people realise to what extent the world is beginning to accept in regard to coal, this process of regulation : people who do not like it of course call it ' improper restriction '. I do not want here to discuss at length the coal problem : coal is productive, sometimes of light, and generally of heat : regulation of coal prices is an issue of considerable liveliness in America, in Germany, and in this country, where a coal Bill is before Parliament at the moment. In fact, since the Act of 1930 great efforts have been made to try and secure a certain steady production of coal, so as to establish first of all a better wage for the miner, and secondly a certain average of price for the community—a much more reasonable arrangement than the kind of switchback economics of high and low prices. In British agriculture much the same policy is being tried.

I would like to ask Professor Hall what his attitude is with regard to restrictive proposals of this character, because it looks as if they will go further ; always bearing in mind that when you come to meat or wheat you are up against greater difficulty than when dealing with tin.

Again Professor Hall touched on the problem of greater agricultural production : we shall want, he said, more butter, more eggs and so on : but he did not refer to a problem present to the minds of a good many of us, the problem of Town *v.* Country in this delightful England of ours. I have the responsibility of presiding over a Royal Commission dealing with this issue. Few people realise how densely peopled England is, that there are 742 people to the square mile, and that it is the most densely peopled country in the world. What is Professor Hall's attitude with regard to this issue ? He spoke of the difficulty of town life, and seemed to contemplate the amelioration of town life by redistribution of people throughout the country. But will not that cut into the productions as well as the amenities of the country ? It is estimated by leading agriculturists that two and a half acres per person is required to support a community. The area available in Great Britain for ploughing, pasture, woods and agricultural productivity generally is under one acre. Are we going to visualise a state of development when the towns are spread more all over the country ? If so, does it not follow as a matter of course that the agricultural productivity is reduced, and if that is so does it not again follow that that must be taken into account when dealing with the economic balance referred to by Professor Hall ?

The third question I should like to ask is this. He referred to Uganda. That is a country which I have the pleasure of knowing well : it is one of the most interesting in the modern world. The great school at Budo, which is called the Uganda Eton, where the sons of native chiefs are trained on public school lines, is one of the finest educational institutions I know of. I am also concerned with industrial and other interests in other parts of Africa. Professor Hall seemed to visualise the development of African agricultural activity as likely to proceed along the lines of world exchange. I quite accept his suggestion that development of native wants is probably desirable and inevitable, but would not from the African point of view a better economy be established if the African acquires wants which can be satisfied by African products, whether grown by European or by Africans ? We all know the immense difficulties of transport overseas and of the exchange, and if development were possible in Uganda, Kenya or Nyassaland, or in Southern Rhodesia of products, if possible new products, which could also satisfy local wants, would not that at any rate from the point of view of the African, secure a better economy than trying to develop small crops of international utility, though those latter might be of some importance from the point of view of the balance of Empire trade.

I speak as one who has in company with others been trying to do something on these lines by introducing the Soya bean, the great Manchurian product, into parts of East Africa, and there is no reason why the Soya bean should not be grown under proper conditions in the British Empire : the Soya bean is a wonderful product and has many utilities : if it can be developed in Africa it would probably provide a form of nourishment for Africans which would be of great utility. It has undoubtedly a value for export with an international market, but I am not at all certain, apart from any question of Empire trade, whether it would not be of greater use in the economic development of Africa if used locally as a sustaining form of soup, or for oil when crushed, and for cattle food, than if it were used merely for international or inter-Imperial commerce.

Professor F. W. FETTER[1]: I very much enjoyed the remarks of your Chairman about Christopher Columbus. Philadelphia is a long way from London, but I shall unblushingly use that story as my own when the appropriate occasion arises. But as the story touches both my professional and national pride, I would like to remind you that Christopher Columbus did discover America.

The question may arise as to why an American should appear

[1] FETTER, Professor F. W.   Professor of Economics in Haverford College, U.S.A.

on the programme of the Royal Empire Society. Presumably one reason is the fact, as so many speakers have well brought out, that the United States and the British Commonwealth of Nations are the two largest economic units in the world, and inevitably their economic fortunes and misfortunes not only react on each other but on all the rest of the world. It seems to me that we have a common interest in trade, in peace and in the preservation of democracy. I find in the United States and in England, in the five months that I have spent here, a very similar attitude towards war. There is none of this sentiment that I sometimes glimpse when I turn my radio to certain Continental stations, that war is an ennobling activity through which the soul of man is purified. It seems to be looked on at best as a dirty business to be undertaken, if at all, only under the pressure of the greatest necessity.

The greater area of the United States makes us seem less dependent upon trade than England. But to a far greater extent than a great many of my own coutrymen seem to realise, some of our most acute economic problems of the last fifteen years have had their roots deep in the international field, and their satisfactory solution can only be got from looking beyond the frontiers of the United States. I assume that one reason why you have asked an American to speak is that he can present the American angle of some of the things taken up, and I shall direct my remarks not only to what Professor Hall has said, but to some of the other economic issues that came up in the earlier meetings.

The recent announcement that negotiations had been opened for an Anglo-American Trade Agreement is a most hopeful sign. I only hope that the forces in the two countries that can take a somewhat broader view of international economic relations can put through a really comprehensive agreement, and not allow those influences which in all countries grow up under the fostering hand of tariff subsidies to render the agreement a meaningless affair. But I am rather alarmed at the tendency shown in the Press to read some deep political significance into the proposed agreement, and to make it out to be democracy's answer to the anti-Comintern Pact. I can imagine nothing that would more quickly arouse opposition to the agreement in many influential sections in the States than suggestions of this sort.

The American public is just now rather sensitive about the idea of again making the world safe for democracy.

It seems to me that any political outgrowth from this agreement ought to be the natural result of its economic effect. That I believe it can be. Professor Hall this morning, and other speakers, have stressed the importance of increased production as the basis for higher living standards. With varied resources and technical skill in the two countries there is a great opportunity for increased interchange of goods on a mutually profitable basis. This extension of trade relations between these two great democracies ought not to be thought of as part of an economic encirclement programme, by which the non-democratic autarchies are to be left to stew in their own juice, but rather as a move toward greater trade and higher living standards in which all are free to participate.

This question of trade restriction has a direct bearing on some economic aspects of the much discussed question of Colonial claims, and of the cries of the so-called " have not " nations to share in the resources of the world. There is a good deal of loose talk on the question of the unequal distribution of resources of the world, resulting from a failure to distinguish between economic ownership of resources and political sovereignty over the land. Unless the present owners were to be expropriated, contrary to existing international law, the annexation of Texas by Italy, or of Canada by Germany, would not mean that the Italians would get their cotton, or Germans their wheat any cheaper than before. They would have to pay the cotton planters and the wool growers for it, just as New Yorkers now pay for their cotton and Londoners pay for their wheat. Given a reasonable freedom of international exchange, every country has access to the resources of the world.

May I suggest that one of the reasons why in the nineteenth century the world looked so complacently on the extension of British sovereignty over so large a part of the earth's surface, was that for economic purposes those sections which appeared on the map in red were about as useful to the citizens of non-Colonial powers as though their own countries had been in control. Since the War, the raising of tariffs within the Empire, the extension of the principle of Imperial Preference, various schemes for the control of raw materials, together with the wave of protectionism in the United States, have somewhat changed the situation. Even with no restriction on the export of raw materials the fact that the great producing countries have high tariffs makes it more difficult for the small countries, and the countries without Colonial possessions, to secure the exchange with which to pay for those products. In a very real sense the easing of trade restrictions and control schemes by those countries which possess the raw materials of the world, brings about re-distribution in an effective economic sense.

Mr. V. C. VICKERS[1]: It is with very great humility that I rise to say a few words, because I happen to be a self-confessed " money reformer ", and have been for some twelve years. I do not wish you to think for a moment that I am here to " spout my own views " or take advantage of an opportunity to " let myself go " on this subject. I desire only to drop a small " brick " in the hope that somebody will pick it up.

We have heard a great deal, and I have listened with the greatest interest, concerning the all-important question of production in relation to consumption, but we have not heard enough, in my view, of the connecting link between them, which is distribution. If we examine distribution we find nothing wrong with our shipping or ordinary transport, but the one prominent thing that does always intervene is " money ". Therefore if money is difficult to obtain and in its availability is entirely out of equilibrium with the volume of trade going on, we are up against a serious barrier to that future permanent increase of trade which we all want so much.

The Chairman well knows that there is nobody in this room more sincerely in favour of the immediate development of the Empire and Empire migration than I am, but I say, as I have said for a long time, that we shall not be really successful under the existing monetary system. We have heard in the last Session and this how the late Chancellor of the Exchequer has been doing a great deal to help things forward ; we have heard him eulogised for introducing " cheap money " and for stabilising prices, and I must say that I believe that to be a tremendous step forward in the right direction. Yet I would also like to

---

[1] VICKERS, Vincent Cartwright, D.L. Director of London Assurance Corporation.

suggest that, at this present time, there is very great and serious opposition to the work that he and the Treasury are trying to carry out. That opposition comes from " Banking and Finance ". The financiers of the world are agitating to get back once more on to some form of gold standard, and to have freedom for foreign lending, to " go back ", and not to " go forward ". We have to watch out for this, and to be very careful to see that suggestions put forward come from disinterested parties and not from people who wish to grind their own axes. Would it be considered reasonable if the Directors of armament companies were the main advisers to the Government as to the number of battleships to be built under our defence programme ? That would be said to be most unfair and unreasonable ; and yet to-day the policy of Government and the legislation of democracy where it involves " Money " is tremendously controlled by " Finance " and those who control Finance.

A few years ago no legislation of great importance involving " money " could possibly go through until the Government had gone to Mr. Montagu Norman and said, "We, the Cabinet, wish to carry out this ; have you any objection ? " He might reply, " You are omnipotent and can do what you like, nevertheless I feel it my duty to say that if you *do* do this, that this, and this, will inevitably happen." Consequently how dared the Chancellor of those days carry out freely what he thought was best for the country ?

We went back to the gold standard in 1925. I know who made us go back, and why we went back ; and the then Chancellor of the Exchequer, Mr. Winston Churchill, has since intimated in public that he was 'badly ' advised. Therefore I suggest that this Conference would not be quite complete unless it took into serious consideration this question of ' money', and the necessity that in future money should be helpful to progress, instead of being a definite hindrance to development, as it is to-day.

Mr. H. HAMEL SMITH[1]: Before I start upon the real cause of my wish to address you, may I give an example of why great care has and will have to be taken in many cases in estimating

---

[1] HAMEL SMITH, H. Editor of *Tropical Life and Stockfarming*. Member Joint East African Board, and West India Committee.

the production of our main crops when comparing them with consumption, in order to prevent excess of stocks. As a writer for the last twenty years and longer on the world sugar market, I may tell you that before the War it was generally estimated and expected that by 1930 we should want 30 million tons of sugar to satisfy the world demand, with an annual increase of one to one and a quarter million tons per annum, according to the increase in population after that. Yet in that year (1930), including India and Russia, only 26 millions were called for, and the last twelve months' estimate will probably work out at 28¼ millions, and this will go on. Competitive attractions have shrunk the demand for sugar products and caused increased demand for tobacco, etc., and this will go on and so some outputs will require to be reduced, and others, probably, increased.

Thus the question of output and distribution must be very carefully watched to avoid scarcity on the one hand and excess stocks on the other. If before the War, we got along easily on the whole, we have got on very badly at times since. The lecturer told us of wheat laid up whilst native masses were starving close by, and rice, sugar, etc., have been accumulated in perfect mountains at times when they were equally badly needed elsewhere. This being the case and common knowledge, I have often wondered why when so many new departments and officials have been appointed a Minister of Production and Distribution, a liaison adviser between outputs and intakes, i.e. consumption, has never been brought into being. Such a Minister has been badly needed for years, but he must be a good man, worth at least £5,000 a year or of no use at all. His word must be above that of the Ministry of Agriculture at Home and of the Colonial Office for Overseas work. How glad also would the Dominions probably be of his advice and opinion, once they felt it worth having, and so if you need good advice, be prepared to pay a proportionately good fee for it. Were such a Minister to be half as efficient as he should be, he should equal the benefit to his fellows of a Bishop of London and a really good man to an Archbishop of Canterbury, and be rewarded accordingly. Only take time to get a man worthy of high pay. Better wait even five years to get what is needed than five years to smother and bury a failure. But within twelve months surely we should find just the man we want.

We must do away on the one hand with the idea of the City luncher after a slightly over-adequate meal, surveying posters urging him to eat more of this, that, and the other until he passes on muttering :

> You can grow your bananas and rice and wheat,
> And the many more crops that are good to eat,
> But 'til camel-like I have " tummies " three,
> How on earth can I eat all you thrust upon me ?

and, on the other hand, of underfed natives in the tropics and elsewhere, where production may or may not be ample and yet food insufficient, even if it exists. The Minister to be appointed must have large-sized maps of the Empire on his tables with a supply of flags to peg places everywhere, including this country. White flags to denote over supplies ; yellow for adequate ; red for below the line of average nutrition, and black for shortage and even starving conditions. With the help of these, his Ministry should have supreme power (to be used tactfully in collaboration with other departments) to move foodstuffs from where they are not wanted or can be spared, to centres where supplies are short or local costs too high. In extreme cases the cost of transport must not be allowed to stand in the way.

In less tragic matters such a Minister could advise centres to take up new crops for home consumption or export, and regulate (not control, which approaches too closely to checking) the flow of the crops generally, foodstuffs or raw materials, much as the police regulate the London traffic. Then, whilst encouraging the smaller resident planters to launch out, or go slow, such as those with an income up to £500 a year—who could be and will be the backbone of increased commerce everywhere—overproduction with unduly low returns, if not actual loss, would be reduced to a minimum, and not only would the producing centres benefit, but also, of course, those firms who cater to supply the necessary machinery, estate supplies and household requirements to them.

In these days with huge corporations and substantially financed concerns owning or controlling vast tracts of plantations and producing centres, there can still be no doubt that for the trade and commerce of the centres themselves, the resident planter is far better as a promoter and supporter of both export and import trading with the merchant firms and manufacturers able to supply such specialised trade. In a word, I vote for a hundred resident planters securing and spending £500 each per annum on an average, rather than for one large concern able to average £50,000 a year, or two firms making £25,000 each, especially as the bulk of those profits are unlikely to remain where produced.

A great help, and often direct encouragement to these smaller resident estate owners, women as well as men (for many women have, and do run estates with success), would be to maintain permanent exhibits of the latest machines, agricultural appliances, locust and pest destroyers, etc., in as many centres as possible, the more the better. The Minister of Production could well take the placing of such exhibitions in hand as well as presiding over committees to choose, buy and send forth those appliances oversea. There must be many cases where the producer and, truly, heaven-sent appliances, never meet. How can they ? The makers cannot send them on approval wide-cast, the planter and cultivator cannot visit every firm, even if he can come to the Mother Country, which many never do. Again, if the machines were on view and not quite suitable for anywhere or for some places, the planter could offer valuable suggestions on alterations to be made, instead of never buying the machine or casting it disgusted on the scrap-heap, and the reputation of every engineer with it, causing curtailment of confidence and trade, to a serious degree.

On the other hand, let machines go out that do the work to a nicety ; the owner cannot be expected to call in his rival producers to come and view that on which much money and anxiety has been expended. Even the makers themselves cannot always tell if a machine, etc., is satisfactory or not, except through the absence of complaints or, more certain still, further orders for a machine ; for a machine that is to go to one estate when dozens would be the better for having it. I believe, before the War, a number of cocoa-drying machines, etc., formed part of such an exhibition at Victoria in the Cameroons, and recently, Lt.-Col. W. L. Julyan, F.R.E.S. addressed a fairly long letter to the *Daily Telegraph and Morning Post*, advocating the introduction of a national agricultural museum in London, for

machinery, tools, etc., to be visited and inspected by farmers
and others over here, as well as planters and stock-farm owners
overseas. Such a museum would be of great help to all visiting
it, but still leave out hundreds of steady-working, progressive
producers who cannot afford the trip home or the costly risk of
importing machinery without being sure that it is exactly what
is needed.

Viscount ELIBANK[1]: I must congratulate the Royal Empire
Society upon having started a series of very interesting talks.
From the address which has been delivered to us at this Session
of the Conference on a subject which is of the most vital importance in considering any economic question which can be
raised, it can be realised how useful this Conference may be.
Only to listen to the very able and lucid address, which opened
the proceedings, is to know that the subject bristles with difficulties, and I could not help feeling as I listened to Professor
Hall that I wished the universe could be as easily moved about
on paper and in practice as Professor Hall was able to move our
minds in the three-quarters of an hour in which he addressed us.
At the same time I could not help feeling like my friend, Sir
Montague Barlow, that the difficulties in practice are far greater
than the difficulties on paper.

I tried in my mind to summarise the main conclusion of that
address, and if I am wrong, Professor Hall will tell me so, but it
seems to me that his solution is, on broad grounds, the intensive
development of the Colonial Empire. That seems to me to sum
up his main theme.

With some experience of development of parts of the Colonial
Empire, I feel that that is not so easy. I do not think that we
take the Colonial Empire and say, " You are merely an estate
and must be developed in this way or that, whether you like it
or not." That has never been our policy. There are a large
number of people in this country who would resist such a

---

[1] ELIBANK, Gideon Murray, 2nd VISCOUNT. Resident Magistrate, etc., New
Guinea, 1898–1901. Native Commissioner, Transvaal, 1900–6. Administrator
of St. Lucia and Acting-Governor of the Windward Islands, 1915–17. Food
Commissioner, West of Scotland, 1917–18. M.P. (Unionist) for St. Rollox
Division of Glasgow, 1918–22. President of the West India Committee since
1930. President of the Federation of Chambers of Commerce of the British
Empire since 1934.

M

policy : I may agree with it in part, but I could not subscribe to it as a whole.

I should like to carry that point further. Sir Montague Barlow put his finger on the pulse of it when he said, " If you are going to develop the Colonial Empire you must do so with the assistance locally of the inhabitants of those Colonies." If you do otherwise, you are at once up against the issue of markets, the real difficulty and crux of the situation. We had excellent examples of that before the War. The last speaker referred to the development of the West Indies and West Africa. I remember very well how hard hit the West Indies were by the development of cocoa by small settlers in West Africa, developed to such an extent that cocoa flooded the markets of the world, the price of cocoa went down, and Colonies like the West Indies who had existed largely on that product, fell into economic difficulties.

It is impracticable to proclaim, " We are going to develop this Colony with this product, and that other Colony with that product, and we are going to help the natives to create wants for themselves." Such a thing does not work out in practice. Markets must be found first.

I come back to what I believe to be the real crux of the matter, and a possible solution. The largest consumers of the world for all products, Colonial and other, are to be found principally in Europe and amongst European races. My belief is that until you have raised the standard of living amongst all European peoples, you will not create sufficient markets to consume the products which you propose to obtain from these tropical places. How to do that is the question we are all asking ourselves every day. There is one sure way, and that is by good trade, but you cannot have good trade unless there is peace in the world, nor can there be confidence unless there is peace. Good trade relies upon peace and confidence.

With reference to monetary reform, one speaker has said that everything rests upon that. I agree that monetary reform may be necessary and has been necessary. The application of money to trade has changed considerably in the last ten years. I agree with him that Mr. Winston Churchill was absolutely wrong when he went back on the gold standard in 1925, but I do not decry the whole of the monetary policy of this country because Mr. Winston Churchill made one bad mistake. I look back further than 1925 and see that in 1914 if it had not been for the then existing monetary policy of this country we should never have survived the War as we did, and come out of it as we did, and indeed as we are doing now. As one who takes a small part in the study and practice of finance, I do not think that you can condemn in wholesale fashion the City or finance because of the conditions in which we find ourselves to-day. Of course the Government has to consult finance and industry if they want to make things go in this country. How could they do otherwise ? This country is dependent upon its industry, upon its export trade and upon what we can produce and sell outside. Unless the Government consults those who are doing these things and who are in industry and in finance, I do not see how they can hope to get the best advice and give the best administration, or secure the best results.

I admit that when you refer to the Empire as a whole—and I speak with deliberation in this matter as one who has visited many parts of the Empire, in fact all the Dominions—that we live to-day in too water-tight compartments as far as these questions are concerned. I do not say that that is the fault of the Dominions : I know that in this country we would gladly go very much further in many respects than the Dominions will go, but you must remember that the Dominions relatively speaking are young : they are growing up but are not yet fully grown, and consequently they are taking the privilege of youth in untying their apron strings. But they cannot absolve themselves from responsibilities that have grown up with them. They are there with huge spaces, some not developed at all, and some not yet properly developed. The eyes of the world are upon these spaces, jealous people and jealous nations, wanting spaces, and unless that is recognised by them, the Dominions are laying up for themselves enormous difficulties. Their interests are our interests, and I think that point alone ought to impress itself upon them, and I should have liked that theme to be developed more fully at this Conference.

I should like if possible to see a Board appointed on which not only this country, but representatives of the Dominions, should be represented, in order to discuss the question of consumption in relation to production. That issue was one of the most important issues discussed in Australia during the general election of two or three years ago, and it is still being discussed there as well as in New Zealand and in South Africa. We should all work together for a solution of that very important issue. I am afraid I have dealt inadequately and somewhat disjointedly with the various nations of which I have spoken, but the time at my disposal has been short and it has not been possible to do otherwise.

Mr. FEATHERSTONE HAMMOND : Lord Elibank has just been talking about this great problem of equalling production to consumption, and he also made reference to Mr. Vickers's criticism of the old money order, which I am happy to say is rapidly dying away, and thought it had a great responsibility in not having elucidated this problem earlier in our history. We have also, in the case of Professor Hall, listened to a discussion on planning to increase both consumption and production, and the very magnitude of the job is enough to make people afraid. If we would only see that what we are trying to do for others they are quite capable of doing for themselves, if left alone to do it, the situation would be easier. When we use money in the way in which it can be useful to us, to express the demand for consumption in the direction in which people are spending their money, goods will be produced to satisfy those demands. Something has been wrong in that there has been great disparity between the purchasing power of the community and the available commodities offered freely on the market for those people to lay claim to. At the Ottawa Conference this Government admitted that something had gone radically wrong and that the first thing to be done was to raise the average index of commodity prices, and when the price level had been raised, it should then be stablised. Stabilisation of prices in a world in which the creative urge is constantly influencing people to produce more and more, means that as fast as commodities come on to a market there is money to buy those commodities, otherwise the price level would tend to fall. If that mechanism is in operation long enough it is the will of the people that will enable them to spend, because that will determine the direction in which to plan. It is the demand which actually has the effect of controlling that planning.

I would direct your attention to the fact that since Mr. Roosevelt has been in power in America the average indices of different prices have been amazingly stable, and production in the United States has been going up continuously, and there has been no cessation in the amount of production in spite of the fact that there have been great falls in export values. Sweden has been following the same policy, and in that case her people have gone from one level of prosperity to another in constant progression ; this year Sweden has a budgetary surplus equivalent to ten million sterling, and is creating a demand for more agricultural products. That is an indication that when money is allowed to perform properly its function it will produce a very different world. It is for the Empire itself to be made a part of this re-organisation on the basis of a stable currency which will make the Empire so prosperous as to demand more people from the home country to help to people an area as fertile as any part of the world. All can be made equally prosperous with the Mother Country if we give them a fair price for the commodities we take from them. When we talk about cash crops, let these be converted into real crops, which will mean that people producing those crops will become the consumers of the goods of the Mother Country.

THE CHAIRMAN (Mr. C. G. Ammon) : I have noticed that everyone has tackled the problem of production. What we would like to know is how we are going to increase the purchasing power of the mass of the people ? That is a difficult problem, especially when we take note of such facts as that for the first time since 1929 we are now producing as much coal as in that year, but 140 thousand less men are employed in producing it. That can be seen in other directions, and it seems to me that to a large extent at home and in the Empire that is the problem we have to face, a problem of which we are apt to be a little afraid.

Sir ARCHIBALD WEIGALL : May I be allowed the privilege on behalf of the Royal Empire Society of offering a hearty vote of thanks to our Chairman, Mr. Ammon, who belongs to a political party that is, I have no doubt, in the minority in this room and in most of our gatherings ? In none of our activities here are party politics allowed to enter, and as an example of this, Lord Snell and Dr. Drummond Shiels are active and extremely helpful members on our Council. In five and a half years, I have never heard them placed in any position of discomfort or disquietude owing to the discussion of Imperial problems in their presence.

In this Session we have maintained the high standard set by my friend, Mr. McDougall, when he opened our Conference with an address on the Dominions. We then went to India, then to the Colonies, and, in the fourth Session, to the world problem ; now we have come to the problem of Production and Consumption.

All I wish to say on the admirable address of this Session is that I am sure Professor Noel Hall does not desire us to consider that out of its proper perspective : it is the ideal which we should keep before us, realising all the time that human feebleness and frailty have to be considered. Those of us who have had to woo electors, who have stood in the House of Commons, who have presided over Governments overseas, who have had to wrestle with a Colony emerging from a Crown Colony to the self-governing stage, will recognise that to put that into practice involves human problems. Make Professor Hall a dictator and he would make your production as elastic as possible, but throughout the British Empire the people own the Government, and the Governments do not own the people.

As Sir Alan Anderson emphasised in our fourth Session, we want to complete the circle of the British Empire as an economic and 'political' unit, using the word in its proper sense. That is our problem and the job with which we are immediately concerned here. If you had told me five years ago that every Dominion and Colonial Government would have pooled resources into a pot in order to give us this amazing building, I should have said it could not be done. Do not let us be frightened to hitch our waggon to the highest star, and hope that we shall get there.

I offer our heartiest thanks to Mr. Ammon and to Professor Noel Hall.

REPLY

Professor N. F. HALL : I hope you will allow me to exclude in my reply reference to the monetary policy.

There is one point on which I was misunderstood. I was not

suggesting that we should aim at any large dependence upon imports in order to raise the standard of life of the Tropical Empire : I was trying to indicate how a relatively small cash crop for export could assist in stimulating economic activity in all sorts of directions by the circulation of a small surplus cash through the whole of the economic system of a tropical colony.

Lord Elibank and Sir Montague Barlow suggested that I was going to make these people dependent on imports for the necessaries of life, but nothing was further from my mind. I was thinking of what happened here when the feudal system broke down. Merchants came here and traded spices in return for wool. This trade involved an inter-manorial circulation of money, an increasing specialisation in production and was the foundation of all our economic development here. We must do the same thing in the Government of the tropical Empire.

When I used the word 'plan' I was using it in its ordinary sense of thinking before you act. I was not advocating ' Planning ' with a capital P along the lines that has found favour in certain Continental countries. I imagined that I should be criticised for my old-fashioned liberalism and my belief in the great value of stimulating individual enterprise. I was, therefore somewhat surprised that one or two speakers have suggested that I rely upon dictatorial and authoritarian methods, and any thought that I might be a dictator was far from my mind. I agree that if statesmen will place their emphasis on policies designed to promote consumption and will choose between the various different types of protection those that do least harm to production, then there are good grounds for looking forward with confidence to the economic future of the Empire. The cardinal difficulty is that the protection of old types of production is relatively easy because there are persons interested enough to ask for it ; there is data upon which policy can be based, there is employment to be safeguarded. But if our policies are based upon improvements in consumption, in some cases none of these factors will be present. We cannot tell how much new employment will be created, how important the new interests will be, how great a contribution they will make to the national income. It is therefore essential that we should devise economic policies which look confidently to the future upon the basis of the historical past ; that we should expect enterprise

and change which have been the means of building the Empire
in the past to be the method of keeping and improving it in the
future.   We cannot stabilise our industrial and economic history
any more than we can stabilise our social and political history.
The danger of our post-crisis policies is the tendency to look back
to the production and trade of the past instead of to the opportunities of increased and improved consumption in the future.

I have been charged with hitching my waggon to a star and
with undue idealism.   It is a charge which I am quite willing
to accept.   The lack of it generally causes a decay in enterprise
and the missing of opportunities.   The value of studying consumption in the past and of wishful thinking for the future
arises from the fact that by that method alone can enterprise
be rekindled and opportunities uncovered.   These are so great
in the Empire as a whole that anyone who is rash enough to
look for them must appear to be idealist indeed!

VI

SOME CONCLUSIONS

Thursday, November 25th. Afternoon Session

THE Right Hon. S. M. BRUCE, C.H., M.C., High Commissioner for the Commonwealth of Australia, had consented to take the Chair, but owing to his necessary attendance at the Brussels Conference as Australian delegate he was unable to do so.

In the absence of Mr. Bruce the Chair was taken by :

Mr. F. L. McDOUGALL : I am very sorry indeed to have to announce that Mr. Bruce is unable to take the Chair at this Session owing to the continuance of the Brussels Conference.

I am perfectly certain that we on our part must regret that he is not with us, even more than he will regret that he is not here. The reasons for our regret are these, that I think there is no statesman in the British Empire who has actually done more than Mr. Bruce to bring to the public mind and the public conscience the idea of increased consumption as a way towards economic peace and Empire development. He was responsible for taking the initiative in 1935 at Geneva on the whole subject of nutrition, and again in 1937 it was he who brought forward the proposal for economic appeasement and for the general enquiry into the problems which governments ought to tackle if they are really going to make the standard of living of the peoples their main objective.

I feel that I have a very heavy responsibility on me in taking his place, and I shall now call upon Mr. H. V. Hodson to give his address.

Mr. H. V. HODSON[1]: My task is to draw together the different threads of the discussions and to weave them into a pattern. It is not an easy task, since the Conference has ranged over so

[1] Editor of the *Round Table*.

wide a field, and has necessarily been driven this way and that by the different views or preoccupation of the various speakers. But I think that four or five main conclusions emerge. The first and perhaps the most important is that the development of the Empire cannot be considered as a problem in self-sufficiency or as isolated from the whole world economic problem. Empire development must be a part of world development. That is a reciprocal relation. As the trade and industry of the world progress, the producers and consumers of the British Empire will benefit. As Empire production and consumption increase, so, if we do not altogether disregard the objectives that have been put forward by almost every speaker at this Conference, world trade will also expand. But the latter somewhat comfortable conclusion ought not to be allowed to degenerate into an excuse for an attempt to develop the economic potentialities of the Empire without regard for the need for better relations between the Empire and foreign countries. Speaking frankly, I feel that such an excuse was part of the apparatus of thought employed at the Ottawa Conference. It has been most remarkable how practical experience since Ottawa has driven into the background exclusive imperial economic policies. I might take Australia as a particular example of the change of attitude. It is a good example, because the Commonwealth has undergone no change of government since 1932. Yet its present outlook, of which you may take Mr. McDougall's address at our first Session as a shining example, is on a very different plane of liberalism of economic thought from the typical Australian attitude of only five years ago.

I might also perhaps be allowed in passing to pay my small personal tribute to the stand taken by Australian statesmen, particularly by Mr. Bruce, against the pernicious doctrine that permanent world economic betterment could be sought in the restriction of production to meet a depressed level of consumption, rather than in the expansion of consumption to meet the enlarged productive capacities which had, for the moment, run ahead of their markets. Somewhat divergent views on the organised restriction of supply have been expressed at this Conference. But so unanimous has been the emphasis on the need for higher consumption that I believe I am expressing the general view in saying that, whatever may be the arguments for organised control as part of the rationalisation of any individual industry, restriction as a universal measure cannot cure depression, cannot solve the major economic problem, and is out of the line of progress towards a higher standard of life for the populations of the world. Personally I would go further, and say that even as regards individual industries there is a grave danger of our identifying the benefit of the industry with the benefit of the British financiers who have invested in it, and to pay too little attention to the welfare of the native workers— the Chinese tin producer or the Tamil coolie on the rubber plantation.

But I am afraid I am wandering too far from my first major point, the relation between world trade and Empire trade. The belief that an improvement in world trade, particularly the trade between the British Empire and foreign countries, is necessary to the sound economic development of the Empire itself has, I think, been one of the outstanding features of this Conference.

But there is a second general consideration that in some degree cuts across this view. And that is that political factors have been and will continue to be important in deciding economic events and in moulding economic policy in the Empire. We cannot altogether stand aside from the economic rearmament that is obsessing the world ; for if war comes, national and imperial economic security may be as vital a part in our defensive strength as in that of other countries. This, of course, is but another argument in favour of the most earnest efforts towards economic appeasement as a contribution to world settlement, since the pursuit of self-sufficiency is bound to be made at the cost of the economic welfare of the ordinary man. I would like in this connection to recall a courageous phrase used here the other day by so hard-headed a political observer as Sir Hal Colebatch. He said that the wealthy countries must be prepared to make sacrifices for the sake of international peace and economic progress. Personally, I would be more timid, and would merely say that wealthy countries must take risks for the sake of peace and economic progress. At our fourth session, Sir John Wardlaw Milne drew our attention to the fact that we need not wait for action on the part of all the smaller nations in order to increase world trade, since one half of it is done by little more than half a dozen of the greatest trading countries.

Besides the political factors, I think this Conference has brought out that there are many social and even moral factors which may modify conclusions that we might draw on the assumption that man is no more than an economic unit. This has particular force, of course, in relation to the Colonial Empire, where we are trustees for millions of people unable to stand by themselves in the strenuous conditions of the modern world, people whose welfare cannot be measured merely by the amount of food they eat, the clothes they wear or the bicycles they ride. Education is an essential part of colonial Empire development, not merely as an adjunct to economic development, but for its own sake. Nothing could be more welcome than the emphasis that Lord Dufferin laid on the fact that exploitation is not the objective even of purely economic development in the British Colonial Empire.

Then there is the question of the impending decline of population in western countries. I bring this in as a social rather than an economic consideration, because I feel that economics are only one aspect of the problem, which is a by-product of our whole social life. After all, it is not the under-nourished, but the over-nourished who are the failing stocks of this country.

A further aspect of economic development into which social factors intimately enter is that of industrialisation and urbanisation. We may feel at one and the same time that along the lines of industrialisation lies the way to economic progress and a higher standard of life in, say, India, and that nothing could be more disastrous than the repetition in India of the by-products of the industrial revolution in western countries in the shape of urban slums and unemployment. I would like to emphasise the need to ensure that progress along such lines is conditioned by a far-seeing social policy, including housing policy.

Let me disgress for a moment in order to bring to your notice the fact that the industrialisation and urbanisation of the oversea Empire are proceeding at such a pace that our old conception of a group of primary producing countries contrasted with a manufacturing metropolis is entirely out of date. Even in New Zealand one half of the population is urban, and in Australia well over half. As regards Canada, where the net output of factory industry has for some years exceeded the net output of all her primary industries combined, even the population of the prairies appears to be moving back to the great manufacturing districts of eastern Canada. We shall be on false lines if we treat the problem before us as if the development of the oversea Empire were only or even essentially a problem of expanding primary production, or as if the terms ' Dominion immigrant ' and ' settler ' were synonymous. Even before the slump the majority of British emigrants to the overseas Empire went into urban occupations, and both in Australia and in Canada the rural population lost at least as much by migration to the towns as it gained by the arrival of new immigrants.

That leads me to the third general point that I think has emerged from our discussions, namely, that economic advance in the British Commonwealth, as a part of the world economic problem, must be made by progress all along the line, from production to consumption, from the agricultural output of the primitive colonial peasant to the technical efficiency of the highly organised industries of this country. The field in which action may be necessary has been shown to include not only production in the material sense but also transport and distribution. The term ' distribution ' has two senses, and both of them apply in this context. It may mean the machinery of wholesale and retail trade whereby goods are transferred from the producer to the consumer. I certainly think there is room for progress there, since one of the basic problems of primary industry is the height of the intermediate costs its products have to bear. While, for example, the producer may be getting only one half of the price he formerly secured for his product, the price to the consumer may fall by only a very small proportion, with the result that the volume of demand is scarcely expanded at all. The question of wholesale markets and retail distribution have clearly to come into our picture.

' Distribution ' in its other sense means the division of the national income among different classes of the population. This also comes into our picture, for in highly developed countries like this it is plain that malnutrition and under-consumption generally are a by-product of a faulty distribution of income, since the wealth of this country should be sufficient to secure an ample standard of life to everybody. Social services are an essential part of the process whereby a better distribution of national income is secured ; hence they, too, must play a part in any programme of Empire development.

Currency, again, has been mentioned, notably by Sir John Wardlaw Milne, and by Mr. Vickers as a vital consideration. It is vital, I think, not for its own sake, but because of the way in which it distributes the forces of production and consumption from time to time. After all, prices are not substantial things, but only a set of numbers, and currency is not wealth but only a means of exchange. Cheap and easy money is perfectly compatible with widespread poverty. But monetary disorder plainly reduces wealth, by leaving productive forces of men and capital idle, and by redistributing income in such a way as to handicap enterprise and defeat the producer, especially the primary producer. Economic progress in a capitalist country is undoubtedly more rapid if the price level is steady or is slightly rising. At the same time, Professor Hall has drawn our attention to the fact that the relation of prices to each other is every bit as important as the general level of prices, and that a rising price level loses its value if it means that Professor Hall cannot have his grape fruit for breakfast, or the working-class child has to go without milk. I would also draw your attention to the fact that the world depression has produced immense economies in costs of production, both in primary and in secondary industries, and that pre-depression price levels are not necessarily the standard at which it is necessary to aim.

I have noted with great interest that there has been no tendency at this Conference to regard migration as an end in itself. To do so is, to my mind, to put on one's hat and gloves before one puts on one's coat and trousers. Migration that is not drawn forth by economic factors is not merely wasteful, it is positively dangerous. While there may be social and political reasons for stimulating migration, the economic reasons can only arise when the economic demand for migrants is already present.

As examples of the wide range that this Conference has shown that action might take, I may perhaps remind you of some of the particular suggestions that have been put forward in our various debates. The list is not comprehensive, but merely a sample. Sir Frank Noyce, for instance, told us what

great scope there was for improvement of the agricultural production in India through the use of better seeds and stock
and agricultural technique. He suggested, as another instance,
that India's welfare might advance if there were a certain
change from grains to other foodstuffs in the dietary and in the
crop system of that country. Several speakers have mentioned
the need for furthering village industries. Mr. Strickland laid
particular importance on the importance of agricultural co-
operation as a means of improving production and eliminating
the costs of the middle-man and the money-lender. Mr.
McDougall mentioned, as an example, what might be done if
the consumption of milk and vegetables in this country could
be raised to a level more closely conforming to an ideal dietary.
There has been reference to better methods of transport, and
incidentally I would lay the greatest stress on the shipping
problem as an element in the economic strength and progress
of the Empire. Miss Esdaile called our attention to the need
for educating and elevating the women of the Colonies. Sir
John Maynard spoke of the need to increase the scale of Indian
agriculture. Sir Alexander Holm referred to the requirements
of the Colonies in the way of capital investment.

This sample catalogue illustrates how different are the problems of different parts of the Empire. The Empire is a world in
miniature, and it would be idle for us to try to find solutions
for the general problem that is before us which would be applicable to the whole Empire and which would go beyond generali-
ties. There is an obvious division between the rich countries
like the Dominions and Great Britain, whose problem is how
to dispose of large productive surpluses either of primary produce or of manufactures, and on the other hand the poorer
countries where the outstanding problem is to raise the standard
of life of the mass of the people to a tolerable level, largely by a
better use and internal exchange of their own resources.

Of course, that is not an absolute or a hard-and-fast distinction. The destitute man is destitute wherever he may be, and his
lot may indeed be harder in a country like this than it is in a
country like India. But the broad distinction remains. It is,
however, a division of the countries of the Empire which has its
greatest force on the consumption side. On the production side
it would be, I think unwise to throw together countries like

India and the African Colonies. For the problem in those Colonies has plainly little or no relation to the problem of industrialisation, which, whatever view we may take of its potentialities, is clearly of vital importance in India and in a few parts of the Colonial Empire. Professor Hall put into our heads some very stimulating ideas on the way in which Oriental industrialisation may benefit the Colonies as consumers, the Dominions as primary producers, and this country as a supplier of high-class manufactured and capital goods. I myself feel that India's economic progress is essentially bound up with the advance of her industrial capacity. I cannot see how the inefficiency of agriculture through the fragmentation of land and the immense pressure of the people on the soil can be avoided save by the progress of industrialisation, whether that means village or urban industries. I do not see in this any lasting threat to India's oversea trade or to our own economic relations with her. If we ask ourselves why trade with India is stagnant, we may point, perhaps, to individual items in her protective tariff, but if we remember that India is a country many times the size by population of any of our European markets, we are bound to say that fundamentally the stagnation of our trade with her is due to her poverty. In the relief of that poverty, rather than in the preferential treatment of any particular industry of ours, lies the best hope for the improvement of our trade with her in the long run.

I have no time to elaborate the divisions into which the countries of the Empire fall in respect of the directions in which their economic development must move. But I think that Great Britain, Australia, India and, shall we say, Nigeria, may be regarded as typical of four main groups. The action that must be taken in these different spheres clearly varies widely. But I would like to end by trying to draw out what is common to the problems of them all.

The first thing, and I think this Conference has brought it home to us, is that the objective of economic progress, the thing on which we must fix our eyes in order to know what our next step should be, is human welfare. The Empire is not a company to be directed for the benefit of shareholders. It is a co-operative concern whose beneficiaries are the people who compose it. In every one of those groups of countries, better nutrition, better housing, better social services are objectives the pursuit of which will lead to progress and to profits on the production side. There must be direct efforts on the production side, of course, because we cannot consume more by merely taking thought, but only by producing more. Nevertheless, consumption, I feel, is to-day the political talisman. At the same time, an essential element in welfare is economic security. I am not thniking only of what has come to be known as social security in industrial countries, but of the wider sense in which every producer, whether an industrial wage earner or a peasant proprietor, wishes to feel that his labour, or his ability to labour, will be rewarded with a fair and proportionate real income. That is very largely a problem of eliminating or mitigating the oscillations of boom and slump. The greatest danger in the economic situation of the world, as I see it at the moment, is the ever-narrowing basis of international trade, which means that every shock is violently and suddenly magnified in its effect on the world price level and on the position of primary producers and the industrial producers for whom they form a market. I therefore return to the point from which I started this address, that in the stimulation of world trade is to be found the most essential means of progress towards Empire economic development. It may be stimulated either by greater freedom of trade, or by more planned trade, or by a combination of both. But unless it is stimulated I believe that our internal efforts may lose a great deal of their effect, and may even be altogether frustrated.

The discussion was opened by :

Sir HENRY PAGE CROFT[1]: I naturally very deeply regret that engagements in the North of England prevented me from being present here at the other Sessions of your Conference, and I would like to congratulate all the promotors of what appears to have been a very remarkable series of addresses.

I have heard a good deal about the subjects which have been delivered and I am most grateful to Mr. Hodson for the admirable summary which he has just given us. May I in the brief

---

[1] CROFT, Sir Henry Page, C.M.G. M.P. (Conservative) for the Christchurch Division of Hants, 1910–18, and for Bournemouth since 1918. Chairman of Executive of the Empire Industries Association. Owner of coffee plantations in Kenya.

N

time rightly allowed to me, endeavour to point just a few directions where perhaps we can help the solution of the great problems which lie before us. I see first of all the need for increasing education amongst the people in this country, in the heart of the Empire, as to what the British Empire really is. I am one of those who devotes, and has devoted, very many years—long over a quarter of a century—to trying to stimulate interest throughout this country, not in Imperialism, not in the idea of a jingo spirit of Empire, but in the belief that it is this great collection of nations which, if properly guided, may be not only a great and lasting benefit to the five hundred million people who dwell under our various flags, but also the great pattern of civilisation which can prove to the world how it is possible for many men of different races, of varying creeds and colours and aspirations to dwell together in harmony and unity as part of one great collective ideal, and as part of one great collective machinery for peace and common defence.

The speaker who has just preceded me very admirably summarised what I understand is the view of members speaking in various Sessions of this Conference, that we cannot ignore the outside world. It is becoming more and more impressed upon all of us how much the world is interdependent. There is only one comment I would make, and it is this, there is nothing that conflicts with that idea of our doing our utmost to see that that quarter of the world where we have influence is healthy. How often we have heard it said that the world cannot progress without a prosperous Russia, or prosperous Germany, or whatever the country may be, and we all know how true that is. How much more true is it that the health and prosperity of territory covering more than one-quarter of the globe, must be secured if mankind is to benefit. How absolutely true it must be that if you can see recovery of great countries like Australia or Canada, and ourselves, that must go a long way towards stimulating the interchange of commodities throughout the world in spite of the high barriers which some nations are erecting around their frontiers.

May I turn to a second point, the question of our not being too reliant upon primary products. As one who has taken an active interest in trying to stimulate migration, I entirely agree with that broad principle. The infiltration of migration for years past has very largely gone into the secondary industries built up overseas. That tendency must go on. There is no good pretending that the migrant is content to be a hewer of wood and drawer of water. We must realise that the greater the wealth in the Dominions the greater will be the demand for products from those and other parts of the Empire. I would offer one comment on that general statement, that I do feel that it is sometimes forgotten in the Dominions overseas that a stimulation to agricultural settlement will be far more likely to give a general uplift to the secondary industries, the transport system and all the services of the Dominion than to be an embarrassment in the matter of over-production. I so largely agree with that, the theory so largely present in people's minds that you must not cut down production, that I suggest that, if it is possible for the primary producing Dominions to welcome schemes of development which might give additional settlement in areas at present sparsely peopled, it would prove to be the most immediate stimulant to secondary industries, and remove many overhead burdens that rest on the Dominions concerned.

I believe that it is true that for every man you can establish on a farm in the countries of the Empire, it means practically two and a half persons engaged in ancillary industries. Therefore do not let us be afraid, provided there is no danger to the labour market of the Dominions, and provided there is no fear of any unfair competition within the Dominion itself, of investing our services or wealth in such ways.

Some of us who have studied the life of Joseph Chamberlain realise how much he was criticised and almost feared when he started out with great programmes of building up new railway systems in various Colonies and different parts of the Empire. When he started on that policy, practically every Crown Colony was a burden to this country, but to-day, except for a brief period during the depression, it can be said of no Colony is that true. Therefore is it beyond the wit of man that we should plan for a possible slump in the days to come, five or six years hence? If it is possible that such a slump may come, should we not start now to plan out great schemes of development, shipping, road transport, railways or aerodromes, in the undeveloped parts of the Dominions, India and the Crown Colonies, also upon irrigation and such great works upon which an expanding prosperity can rely in the days to come ? I throw that out as a subject upon which one can dwell at length, but I am convinced that it is not an unwise and selfish policy that we should try to educate the City of London to see that its surplus wealth goes to build up the Empire overseas. If we consider ourselves as a great landlord, it is our duty to see that our estate is developed, and that we may not delay in bringing about the development of our Empire.

I read a lot of letters in the newspapers where it is suggested that the British Empire is selfish, that we in this country adopt a dog-in-the-manger attitude. I beg that the leaders of imperialism who have been at this Conference may set to work in order to undo this kind of mischievous statement. It is, I think, within something like the last eighty years, that nearly nine-tenths of the people of the British Empire have either become self-governing or are in process of becoming self-governing, and how can anyone say that that is a selfish policy ? Get rid of the idea that Downing Street controls the whole of the British Empire, and that people living overseas are under a kind of tutelage. Wherever a country has approached the possibility of self-government, we have been ready to make it possible, and when we see people suggesting that in order that we may remove the frowns from the brows of dictators, we should hand over one part of the British Colonial Empire to some international body not stated, which has no experience of Colonial administration, let us get rid of this inferiority complex, let us realise how fine our adminstration has been, let us intensify our efforts and prove conclusively to the rest of the world that we are just in our stewardship and doing all that is humanly possible for mankind under our trusteeship.

The discussion was opened by :

Mr. A. A. SOMERVILLE : May I make a suggestion ? There have been two conferences, one at the Guildhall[1] and this remarkable conference, and the object of the two conferences has been the same. The first was a popular appeal to the people here to take into consideration the urgent need to develop the Empire. This, as it seems to me, has been a conference with a

---

[1] Conference on Empire Migration, held in the Guildhall of the City of London, October, 1937.

platform for testing ideas and putting in a well-argued scientific way the possibilities of development.

Two matters were mentioned by the principal speaker at this Session with which I cordially agree. One is the interdependence of trade all over the world, and the other is the necessity for remembering that it is no good trying to have artificial migration. It must be migration that is naturally stimulated by development.

The suggestion I would like to put before Sir Archibald Weigall is this : Are we going to separate without any practical result from these two conferences ? Is it not possible to form a Standing Committee of those best qualified to undertake the work to follow up what has been said and done at these conferences, and to find means of forming public opinion. If such a Committee were formed—and there is no body or centre so well-fitted as the Royal Empire Society, and this building for such a centre—we might then get a centre that would carry on the work which might be of inestimable value in the great work of developing the Empire.

Mr. SOMERSET DE CHAIR : I was sorry that Mr. Stanley Bruce was not able to be in the Chair this afternoon, although that casts no reflection on the admirable chairmanship we have had, for it was partly because Mr. Bruce was the first Prime Minister I ever heard speak, that I became particularly interested in Empire politics. I remember listening to him in the Australian House of Representatives at Canberra the day that the new Parliament building had been opened, and I remember marvelling at his golden voice and wonderful statesmanship. I think that possibly it was the spectacle of Mr. Bruce that first turned my mind towards a political career myself. I should like to have been able to thank him to-day for the inspiration he gave me so long ago.

In the shifting world where we live to-day I often feel that the Empire is the only real thing left ; it is the only stable thing : we see the old landmarks in Europe going, nations warring against one another, dictators shouting at each other, and the world seems to be disintegrating before our eyes. But aloof and apart from this changing, colourful kaleidoscope, you have the Empire, something real and something solid, an Empire in which there are 500 million inhabitants, a quarter of all the human souls on earth, and those people living under the British flag enjoying peace, good relations, stability and a steadily developed standard of life. That is something worth preserving in a decaying world, and that is why I feel that this Conference and the one at the Guildhall, have done so much to rivet attention on something which is really valuable, and to divert our minds from the more alluring, but very much less useful distractions on the Continent.

I was very interested in Mr. Hodson's point about the growing urbanisation of the Dominions, and that is a point hardly recognised in England. In New Zealand, he said, over half the population were urban, and he said that in Australia considerably more than half are urban. I think he understated it, for in Australia out of a population of 6½ million, only half a million are engaged upon the soil. The enormous proportion of the population there live in big cities, and therefore their whole outlook is covered by the development of secondary industries, and life in big cities. That must be realised in this country in considering Empire problems. There is an equally interesting fact of which the Dominions understand little, that the biggest agricultural production in the Empire is the agricultural production in the British Isles itself. It may be news to some of the Dominions that there are more people engaged in agriculture in Great Britain than in any of the Dominions, and that the agricultural output is greater than that of any of the Dominions, greater than that of Canada, or Australia ; and the other Dominions fall far behind. That is a problem which I think is not understood in the Empire, that we have this enormous agricultural production in England which must be safeguarded when there is a question of selling food in the English market.

We are now confronted with a new development in Imperial policy which may have vital effects on agricultural production in England and the Dominions—the Anglo-American Trade Agreement, and, while I am one of those who believe that a great access of prosperity may come from a genuinely reciprocal trade agreement with the United States, a new prosperity which may come into the breach when the armament programme here begins to flag, and may have an important effect in maintaining the existence of our industry, I should like to be well assured that we are not going to be led into a trap. Because there is a danger that this idea of a trade agreement, which is perfectly genuinely held in the White House, may not be shared by the mass of Americans. Mr. Cordell Hull is a man of great idealism and is anxious to see a genuinely reciprocal agreement with this country, but behind the White House is that vast hinterland of the United States, the Middle West, and we want to be assured that we are not going to find ourselves making considerable sacrifices to the United States, in a reciprocal agreement which in the next Presidency may be repudiated by the vast bulk of the American people. That is a matter that we should watch carefully. Certainly I have every confidence in our Government, and know that they will watch over the interests of the Empire and agricultural producers in this country, but it would be a pity if, in default of any expression in the country, they should feel that there is no anxiety as to what the *quid pro quo* may be.

We know that the real problem in the United States is the problem of their agricultural produce, and the great idea of the agreement on their side is to find somewhere to dump their surplus agricultural produce, which they have tried to restrict under the A.A.A. If we are to be faced with increased agricultural produce coming into this country we must have a guarantee that our own market will be maintained. That is a point where Dominion and British agriculturalists meet on common ground. Some interesting information was given in the House of Commons as to what it would cost in terms of subsidy to maintain agricultural prices in this country on a fairly high level, and it was revealed that in order to provide the following prices :

Wheat, 50s. per quarter ; Sugar beet, £40 per ton ; Barley, 45s. per quarter ; Oats, 24s. per quarter ; Beef, 50s. per cwt. ; Milk, 1s. 2d. per gallon (12 months average) ; Mutton, 1s. per lb.

It would require £21 million only per annumn over and above the market prices now received.

If the Government could assure the agriculturalists in this country that in this Trade Agreement with America, there would not be any danger to agriculture, I believe a great anxiety would be lifted off the agriculturalist in this country.

Lt.-Colonel WALEY COHEN : I rather wanted to say a word on the lines of Mr. Somerville's remarks. I am interested in the practical issue of these Conferences and I do not think that we can do better than take the lines indicated at the previous session, that we do want to decide upon the star to which we wish to hitch our waggon. I am a farmer too, and I should be very sorry to see this great Society dispersing its efforts on all the general questions of trade that are dealt with by numerous economic and other organisations in this country. It would be well if, as a result of this conference, whatever is done should concentrate on the Imperial side.

There is one thing which has not had a place in our discussions, and that is the enormous importance of public order throughout the British Empire. I do not know if any of you had a chance of realising the temporary effect of what may be called the absence of public order in the Mediterranean during the last few months, on prices and on trade generally coming through the Mediterranean, but if you have, you will understand how very necessary the steps taken by the British Government were, and how very great is the danger to trade, particularly Empire trade, of any disturbance of public order throughout the British Empire and in fact throughout the world. We do not know yet what will be the result of the terrible disturbances in China and Japan to British and general trade. These two instances I think do emphasise the enormous importance of what I may call public order throughout the world.

A good deal has been said about nutrition, and about the distribution of food. Some of you have read the report of the Committee which has been sitting and discussing the distribution of milk in this country, but it is necessary not to be too narrow. One of the points on the nutrition question is as to the relative value of powder milk and pasteurised milk as food. One of the great difficulties in discussing the nutrition question is to keep up to date with the enormous developments that are going on, and if I may repeat what was said by Professor Hall, I think we want to be very careful to keep our eyes looking forward, and not to be too much obsessed by practices and systems in the past.

There is only one exception I should like to make, and that is on the question of migration. I quite agree that to stimulate migration when there is no occupation or demand for the migrant is courting failure, but I want to remind you that it was not until Edward Gibbon Wakefield came along that the possibility of migration to New Zealand on a large scale came to the fore, and what we have to do is by development to stimulate those openings and the demand for labour to migrate. From 1901 to 1913 there was a great movement of migration. That was made possible largely by an enormous transfer of capital that flowed to various parts of the Dominions. What we now have to do is to try and find out what possibilities there are for the movement of capital so as to create the possibilities for employment of migratory labour. In this connection I would like to draw your attention to the old Colonisation Board which obtained its funds by the sale of land in the Dominions before the Dominions came into being as such, and they spent the money partly in development, and partly in helping out migrants. Over a period of seventy years the experience was the same, that for every migrant whose migration was assisted from public funds, four others at the lowest, and sometimes seven went out at their own expense.

Believing as I do, that one of our great troubles in this country is density of population, and agreeing entirely that it is hopeless to send out people when there is not an opportunity and a demand for them, one of the problems I should like this Empire Society to devote itself to, is the finding out of how capital can be transferred and how these openings can be created in the Dominions. Then I think many of the advantages suggested as regards world trade, would follow in due course.

Mr. CHARLES H. LUKE : Mr. Hodson stated in his able address that the matter of migration could not be stimulated except by the economic urge. I should like to ask him if he and those who agree with him think that there is sufficient economic preparation to create that economic urge ? During this conference I have not heard any reference to the statement published in the *Times* four years ago in the form of a letter, signed by four Members of Parliament, in which they advocated and set forward a scheme for the economic preparation of the uninhabited parts of the world by the aid of loans provided by the consent of the Dominion or country concerned, by this country, the wealthiest member of the British Empire. Not one word has been said about that scheme in recent years, but I am one of those who hold that there is something wrong with our development of the Empire so long as we do not go in for economic preparation to induce migrants, in order to make a better distribution of the white population of the Empire, the present mal-distribution being a menace to the peace of the world and of the Empire.

Miss C. G. K. SCOVELL : I come to this platform with much diffidence in view of previous distinguished speakers and after Mr. Hodson's brilliant summing up.

But I hope it will not be too late to put shortly one point of view, and to make a practical suggestion with which any Committee formed after the Conference may feel inclined to deal.

In this matter I am speaking also for some of the younger men with property and business interests in Africa, too busy to attend conferences, but who feel that the African (especially in our Eastern Colonies) is not getting a fair deal—that there is a great potential market which cannot be developed until the consuming and working power of the native African is improved Better health and education are needed also before you can get exports or any improvement in production and trade.

Surely Lord Dufferin was wrong when he said that " without export trade there could be no money for hospitals or schools ", for as long as people suffer from diseases which prevent mental and physical efficiency, there is not likely to be much to export.

Much has been said about poverty and malnutrition, but nothing about the preventible disease and bad sanitary conditions which undermine the stamina of the Native peoples and keep the African a poor man because an unhealthy one. These diseases could be stamped out and prevented by more determined efforts, but need a certain amount of capital expenditure, which young Colonies cannot be expected to provide out of revenue. I suggest that we are not making right use of the Colonial Development Fund, very little of which has hitherto been spent directly on preventive Public Health work. May I press, to begin with, for a further allocation of £500,000 for this Fund in the 1938 Colonial estimates, to be spent on this most urgent work. If the capital needed could be advanced by the

Colonial Development Fund on *short-term* loan, interest plus sinking fund could be paid. Possibly it would be advisable to set aside 10 per cent for grants outright in special cases.

As time is short, I will only give three typical instances in illustration—from the 1935 reports, the latest available.

First from *Zanzibar*, where the infection rate from hookworm is estimated at over 80 per cent among the general native population, with a higher rate still among the children in rural areas.

In *Kenya* the Medical Officer of Health says that a Medical Survey in 1931 showed that one whole tribe was in danger of ultimate extinction through one disease only, and adds, " Nothing is known of the interval 1931–5, as there has been no money either to take preventive measures or to repeat the survey." This Medical Officer also speaks of the necessity for research if money is to be well spent, and speaks of the fine laboratory building at Nairobi without endowment or staff to do the necessary work.

In *Tanganyika* the Bishop this year advertised on the Wireless, to the world in general, England's shortcomings in the matter of prevention and treatment of malaria. His appeal brought in £5,000 to be spent on quinine necessitated by the lack of adequate preventive work by the Government. Each Colony has its own problem, equally urgent. Can we afford to ignore them ?

I make no apology for repeating the words of our Chairman at the opening Session—" the key of production should be the best human being "—and I would like specially to support the plea for better education of the native women. Public Health begins in the home, and ultimately comes back to the efficiency of the mothers of the race. For this education, women doctors and women trained in sanitary, welfare work, and midwifery, are necessary, to visit and explain to the mothers *in the home*, while their children are being taught in the schools along the lines of Dr. Paterson's admirable *Book of Civilisation*.

Mr. MUNRO ROGER : It is almost presumption on my part, after hearing such a galaxy of experts, to intervene at all in this discussion, but my practical experience in this question here and on the Continent may be of some value.

One very important feature of this attempt at world appeasement, particularly European appeasement—the appeasement
of the Dictators— has been overlooked. It is a psychological
one. I have studied it very closely, sitting in hundreds of cafés
and otherwise closely mingling with the people of half a dozen
of the most important countries of Europe. I have watched
the people, measured their standards, studied their mentalities
and their outlook compared with our own. I could discern no
desire or intention to respond to our " generous gestures ", but
to take all we could give them as their right. I was living in
Brussels when we introduced our tariffs. The Belgians were
positively rude to English people. They asked how dare we
keep their goods out of our markets ? I answered—for the very
good reason that many of our industries were nearly ruined,
while they had been living in prosperity on our markets for
sixty or seventy years.

We must not lose sight of this important consideration ; we
must not be sentimental about that agreement with America ;
we must not, as usual, sacrifice our own people. As Mr. de Chair
said, we must be alert and wise. Who should we consider first?
—our distressed areas, and the general pressure on our Nation,
or the people we sentimentalise about in other countries ?

Can you visualise the Empire that might have been developed
if we had had Cabinets with vision and courage in the past and
a more practical outlook and determination to utilise our vast
potential resources on the part of our present Cabinet ? We
must not forget that Cabinet Ministers are not gods, but men,
and think and act for ourselves. Think of an Empire of say
200,000,000 of British people, instead of the present miserably
weak 20,000,000 outside these islands ! What great markets
could not such an Empire have developed for ourselves and for
the world ? What powerful auxiliary Navies could they not
have possessed to co-operate with ours ? Would Dictators
threaten as they do now ? We could then, without anxiety and
further terrible sacrifices, in conjunction with our friends of the
United States of America, easily preserve the peace of the
world.

Foreigners do not understand our extraordinary neglect of
our Empire. A German official visited our distressed areas some
time ago. He reported publicly on his return that they were

infinitely worse than he expected and he failed to understand how they could exist in a Nation that possessed such an Empire as ours.

I have spoken on the Empire question here and in Scotland and have been appalled by the ignorance on the subject I found everywhere. I have discussed it with Members of Parliament who did not seem to know the elementary considerations in the Indian question, for instance. This ignorance is dangerous, and the greatest efforts should be made to remove it.

It is our first duty—and we should have realised it long ago —to ensure that such possessions as have been bequeathed to us by our ancestors should be developed for the benefit of our people, the descendants of those ancestors who made the Empire at heavy cost. And what a magnificent Empire could we not make of it, with developments that would benefit our own people and the whole world beyond our present conceptions !

Our Navy and our Army have to be increased and maintained. We can only do this without an intolerable and dangerous strain by a real practical, whole-hearted development of the almost incredible resources of our Empire. Let us do our duty to our own people first and make common-sense use of those resources. Let us realise what it means to our future. Let us strengthen ourselves basically and we will help the world more effectually than in any other way.

Lord BLEDISLOE : I have already spoken during this Conference, but there is one point made by an eloquent and well-informed speaker à propos of emigration to which I should like to refer. " Migration ", he said, " is not an end in itself. It depends on economic demand." He went on to say that he would carry it a little further and ask : " How is that economic demand to be stimulated ? " I think that the answer was given by Sir Henry Page Croft when he said that in the British Empire we have a great inheritance which required development. Without capital to develop it, it could not possibly be developed or inhabited.

Some of you know that I have come recently from New Zealand. That is a country which is pre-eminently crying out for British capital. If British capital were available, there are plenty of rich natural resources in New Zealand waiting for development, which if developed with British money now lying on deposit at our Banks and yielding no more than one per cent, can with perfect confidence under able British industrial management yield at least 6 per cent.

I hope that we are not going to leave this Conference without some definite plan of what we mean to do. Colonel Waley Cohen has put a very important question, which I want to answer, and it is in effect, What is the Government going to do and what are we as individuals going to do ? I believe that we can do at least as much as, if not more than, any Government. New Zealand, the most attractive country in the whole of the Empire, is crying out for population and capital to develop her economic resources and provide for her adequate defence. I do earnestly suggest that before we press the Government to do anything further, those in the City of London who can provide the capital and the business skill and acumen, to give a real stimulus to increased migration overseas, will do their part, and I feel sure that if they do, the Government will not be slack in doing theirs.

The other day I went on a deputation with Mr. Somerville and others to the Prime Minister, with a view to asking that the British Government should give a lead in this matter of migration. We have been reminded by several speakers from this platform that as the result of the Statute of Westminster the Dominions have become completely autonomous. But it does not follow that they do not welcome a lead from the Old Country, and I would go so far as to say, having taken great pains to study meticulously the attitude of one at least of the self-governing Dominions overseas, that nothing is more calculated to stimulate their patriotic and Imperial activities, viewed from the development standpoint, than a sound, clear and emphatic lead from the Old Country.

REPLY

Mr. H. V. HODSON : I think perhaps I had better start by taking up what I may describe as Lord Bledisloe's challenge. First let me correct his opening remark. I did not say that migration might not be an end in itself. I simply noted that there had been no tendency in this Conference to refer to it as an end in itself. My personal view is that it may be sometimes an end in itself on social grounds. It is not so much a question of the comparative standard of life that the individual may have in this country or in Overseas Dominions, as of the opportunities he may have to make the most of the talents that are in him.

That question of equality of opportunity is primarily a social rather than an economic factor.

There are two ways in which we can regard the migration problem. We may say that we do not like the present distribution of population and would like it to be otherwise for reasons concerned with that population itself, and that we must aim, therefore, at those economic conditions which will produce the migration we regard as necessary. Or else we may pursue independently an economic programme, and if it results in migration that fact will show that migration is an economic advantage.

What should we do, then, if we wish to promote migration? I agree with the speakers who have told us that capital is the first requisite in the conditions of to-day. As regards Government loans, there is a great difficulty. Australia and New Zealand, the principal Empire borrowers of British capital for public purposes before 1929, found during the depression that the load of their Government debt was such that they firmly set their face against increasing it. My answer to the question, what was done in response to the appeal made by Lord Tweedsmuir and others, is that of Australia, New Zealand and Canada, the three Dominions who provided the main field for migration before the depression, Canada is at present out of the picture because of the enormous amount of its own unemployment at present. I was reading figures recently which show that now that migration from Canada to the United States has stopped, Canada would be more than able to supply her own population needs for five or ten years to come even if the high rate of economic expansion prevailing in the twenty years before 1931 were restored. It would need something quite exceptional in the way of economic expansion to create a need for immigrants. Australia and New Zealand are different, and I think it is in that direction that we should concentrate our ideas.

Where is capital development to go? Sir Henry Page Croft

urged that it should be put into primary production. This may be mining, into which capital is already going in considerable quantities. But agriculture raises a rather more difficult problem, because although there may be a market for a certain amount of extra produce from the Australian countryside in Australian cities as they develop, yet that home market has not yet come anywhere near providing for any of the major products of Australian agriculture or pastoral industry. It is, therefore, essentially a question of overseas markets. Where is Australia to find them ? Are those markets to be found here ? That brings me to the question raised by Mr. de Chair, that of British agriculture. The relation between British agriculture and the agriculture of the Dominions seems to me to be a vital question which has not been really thrashed out. What is the nature of the market for British agriculture ? (I except wheat, because wheat has been put on a satisfactory footing, and the fact that it is satisfactory is largely due to the small proportion of the total of wheat consumed in this country that we produce ourselves). The markets for other products are largely dependent upon a rising standard of life in this country. If you consider the household budgets of people at different levels of income, from the very poor to the very rich, you find that an increasing proportion is spent on home food products as you go up the scale. Poor people, who cannot buy fresh milk, buy tinned milk from overseas. People up to the upper middle class buy imported meat. Hence there can be no solution for the problem of home agriculture except in economies of cost, with the aid of subsidies or otherwise, which will bring the prices down to meet existing levels of income, or else in an increase in the amount of money available for spending on agricultural produce by the poorer classes of this country. It is there that we shall find the solution, because we shall then see that there is plenty of room for the specialised cheap products of the Dominions, as well as the higher class fresh products of this country.

That brings me to another point that has been raised—the depressed areas. There are depressed areas everywhere. The so-called Special Areas are geographically segregated ; but within half a mile of this Hall you could find a depressed area, and that is the essential problem. Those concentrated special areas exist because of the decline of international trade.

Tyneside and South Wales have been dependent in the past on shipping, ship-building, coal exports and the whole flow of international trade, that is another reason why we cannot divorce the British agricultural problem and the Dominion agricultural problem from the larger problem of world trade.

Mr. F. L. McDOUGALL : Before asking Sir Archibald Weigall to do two things—to reply to the several questions we are going to put to him and to propose a vote of thanks to the speaker, there are one or two remarks I would like to make.

I think it is an extremely good thing that Mr. de Chair raised to-day this picture of the relationship of British and Overseas Empire agriculture so far as the United Kingdom markets are concerned. I believe the answer is that the problem that Mr. Hodson has indicated is the correct one. To take one instance : during this year, 1937, the average price of New Zealand lamb has been $7\frac{1}{2}d$. The average price for home killed lamb has been somewhere about 1s. 2d. These two figures make it really clear that if you are to get an increasing market in the United Kingdom for the extremely high quality United Kingdom products such as home killed meat, you must build up the purchasing power of the people very considerably.

One or two things follow perfectly clearly. In this market there is an enormous demand for an increased consumption of the very sound good products from the Dominions which may not have quite the reputation of home-killed stuff, but if you take such things as beef and butter, meat and fruit, it is quite clear that there are really two markets. the high quality market and the market for 60 or 70 per cent of the population really catered for by imports.

I am quite sure that the whole Conference, not only those present to-day, but those present each day, would like me on their behalf to turn to Sir Archibald Weigall, and the Secretaries and say how grateful we are to them for having had this really bright idea of holding a Conference on Empire Development from the standpoint of consumption and production. I think all our discussions have tended to show how wise it was of the Royal Empire Society to take this initiative. I think we have come to the conclusion that if it is possible to find means whereby consumption can be increased and stimulated, the

o

results will be increased production, with most beneficial effects on trade and migration.

This is the question I would like to put to Sir Archibald Weigall :

What are you really going to do about what we have been discussing ? We all know how easy it is to discuss a problem, but how difficult to find an opportunity to follow the suggestions even when they have been well framed. Therefore, we would very much like to know how the Royal Empire Society itself would propose that the discussions initiated here, and which have aroused so much interest, should be followed up.

Finally I should like to say that I am quite certain that the discussions of this Conference have shown that the British Empire has a very great opportunity in front of it, of doing two things—finding means of concerted action among its own members to improve the general measure of prosperity of all its people, and at the same time of making a very great contribution to the future prosperity of the world, and in that way doing something which in my opinion will go further to ensure world peace than anything else.

Sir ARCHIBALD WEIGALL : Before I answer this question may I be allowed to make two observations on what Lord Bledisloe and Colonel Waley Cohen have said. I of course accept with Lord Bledisloe that there are industries in New Zealand which will return in one case 6 per cent on an investment, and in the other case 10 per cent. I cannot conceive that if Lord Bledisloe with all the authority that he possesses as an ex-Governor-General, goes into the City of London and says, " Here are these investments. Why don't you go and use your capital which is only producing 1 per cent at these greatly advanced rates ? " that any private capitalist would be prevented from doing so.

Colonel Waley Cohen said, " What is the Royal Empire Society going to do ? " He suggested that we should bend our minds to try to increase the investment of capital in the Dominions and give a stimulus thereby to economic development to be followed by automatic migration. I do not pretend to speak for New Zealand, but I know something about Australia. May I recount an experience I had ten years ago. I was Chairman of a small Syndicate, who raised a few thousand pounds to examine and explore the question of a chilled meat industry in Australia. The idea was an expenditure of several millions on building special ships and the development of territory which, in the opinion of experts sent out, was capable of carrying out this great work. The first question I was asked in the City of London when I asked for ten million was, " Yes, but on one condition, that we enjoy the fee simple of the land." I mentioned the Statute of Westminster, but the State Government said, " No, it is our definite policy that we cannot sell the freehold. You can have a leasehold." This, of course, was not sufficient security, and this is an actual fact that happened less than ten years ago, and shows that it is not so easy. After all, the Government of a Dominion presumably must be allowed to know its own business best.

Let us get down to the real question that affects us now the Conference is ending. What is the Royal Empire Society going to do ? In the first place this in only the end of a chapter and not the end of a book. As a result of a consultation I had last night with Professor Newton, who edits our well-known series of Imperial Studies, we have decided to publish the verbatim report in book form, after the several speeches have been submitted to the speakers, and that will go out widely in this country and all over India and the Dominions for their information and enlightenment. It will cost a certain amount, but we have made arrangements for that expenditure.

What has happened in this Society up to now is this. We have great monthly evenings where the speaker of the moment on the subject of Empire interest has opened a full dress debate, and we have had contributions which have made for nothing but good. The last two of these evenings both had to have closed doors as far as the Press were concerned because the big speakers would not come unless the Press were excluded. We had a tremendous discussion on Palestine by Sir Horace Rumbold, in which Lord Samuel, and Dr. Weizmann took part, and a little while ago we had an address by Sir Frances Lindley on the events in the Far East followed by a debate of immense interest.

I have been Chairman of the Royal Empire Society for nearly six years, though it is only a two year appointment, it has fallen to me and to the Secretary to arrange all these Conferences, the monthly meetings and our luncheons. The library has increased enormously, and now contains 300,000 volumes. The newspaper room has 700 new papers every day from all over the Empire. It should not be left to the control of the Secretariat here and a humble and inefficient chairman like myself. What we do propose to do is this. As a result of this Conference I am going to ask some of those who have taken part if they will come and meet us here, and to form a standing Committee such as was suggested by Mr. Somerville, to continue this work of real Imperial interest, and I hope, education throughout the whole of the Empire. These are specific works that have arisen out of this Conference.

I was enormously impressed with the small impromptu speech which the High Commissioner for India made here following Sir Frank Noyce. He said, " Take care that India does not become for you another Japan, and therefore a competitor to the industries of other countries because of the low cost of labour and low standard of living." The only way to create a fair balance of trade between India and this country in the future is by increasing the standard of living amongst our millions in India.

We have our Branches in India. We had a travelling Commissioner out there last year, and there is a work that I want stimulated from here. Our Fellows in India are co-operating with the educated Indians to try and devote their minds to the work.

I only hope the Standing Committee will help us to make much more use of our incomparable library than is now made.

It is a horrible thought, that in no one single University throughout the whole country is there any Chair of Imperial Relations. There is not a single Chair whose holder has devoted himself to discussing the enormously changing problems of the whole inter-Imperial relationship under the Statute of Westminster. That is a problem that is connected with everything we have discussed here.

One speaker asked, " What is the British Empire, and how will it work in the future ? " The answer to that question is one that can only be given after a good deal of really close examination, because under the Statute of Westminster it is perfectly possible now for the Ministers of the King of South Africa to give different advice on a great question of foreign policy to that given by his Ministers to the King of Australia. That sort of problem has not been tackled and I do suggest that here in our library we have unique ammunition for tackling that problem, and we are in a position of Commander-in-Chief for a huge munition dump of high explosives and no guns to fire them off. I want to see a Standing Committee able to fire that ammunition for the enlightenment of everyone all over the Empire.

In conclusion I want to express our heartfelt thanks to Mr. McDougall and Mr. Hodson and the permanent officials of the Secretary of State for the Dominions and the Secretary of State for the Colonies, and to those we owe a real debt of gratitude.

I have only been the donkey boy to do a certain amount of donkey work, but it is to them our thanks are really due not only for what they have done this afternoon, but for what they have done in the initiation and arrangement of this Conference.

APPENDIX

December 2nd and 3rd, 1937

AFTER the close of the principal Conference, whose sessions have been recorded in the preceding pages, a new and unprecedented series of discussions was arranged in which those who could not take part with their elders might have the opportunity to ventilate their ideas on the same problem. By reason of their influence among persons of their own age and standing it was felt that they should be afforded the chance of taking counsel together.

At the invitation of the Council of the Royal Empire Society a private Conference of more than eighty young men and women between the ages of eighteen and thirty-five from many parts of the British Commonwealth met on December 2nd and 3rd, 1937, to discuss in outline the economic and other problems of the Empire. The members were drawn from the universities of the United Kingdom and of the Empire oversea, and both undergraduates and post-graduate research students received invitations. There were also members coming from business, professional and missionary circles, and many phases of opinion were represented. Members both of European and non-European stock took part in the Conference.

It was unanimously decided by those present that in all published reports of the proceedings of the Conference and of any discussion groups arising from it all contributions should remain anonymous.

In the first Session the economic problems of the Commonwealth were considered under four headings : (*a*) the internal problems of the Commonwealth countries ; (*b*) the interrelation of economic policies within the Commonwealth ; (c) the international implications of Commonwealth policies ; (d) the economic future of the Commonwealth. With an eye both to the present and the future the term ' Commonwealth ' was interpreted as meaning " the comity of self-governing nations which owe allegiance to the British Crown together with their respective dependencies ".

The discussion was opened by two young experts, one of whom came from the United Kingdom and the other from Canada, and although their opinions were conservative and radical respectively, they showed almost complete unanimity on the points raised in the agenda and in the final resolution which is reproduced below. Thirteen other members spoke at this Session—representing the United Kingdom, Canada, Australia, New Zealand, South Africa, Northern Rhodesia and the Gold Coast. There was voiced in the contributions a great diversity of opinions, but it was the happy lot of the rapporteur to record an impressive degree of unanimity which was ulti-mately expressed in the Conference resolution, decided upon at the fourth and last session.

The whole of this resolution on matters economic had a bearing, direct or indirect, on the twin questions of production and consumption. It ran as follows :

" That this Conference is substantially agreed :

(i) That the leading economic policies of the Governments of the British Commonwealth should aim at promoting with all the resources under their control better nutrition and a higher standard of living among all British subjects, and that in so doing the Governments should give equitable treatments to both white and coloured populations.

(ii) That the Governments should work persistently for freer trade within the Commonwealth as a step towards freer world trade in capital and commodities alike, and that the pending trade negotiations with the United States of America are to be regarded as a move in the right direction ;

(iii) That the organisation of economic opportunity should precede the resumption of a large-scale emigration within the Commonwealth ;

(iv) That autarchic policies, whether for the Commonwealth or for its individual units, are to be avoided and the idea of exclusive trade preferences rejected ; and

(v) That improved facilities are urgently needed for obtaining a more comprehensive knowledge of economic possibilities throughout the Commonwealth."

At the second, third and fourth sessions other problems of the Empire-Commonwealth—constitutional, political, social and cultural—were discussed. As was inevitable, certain questions of method on which there was a division of opinion had to be set aside for further study and discussion, but the impression which an impartial observer carried away from the Conference was that of a general awareness of the vital issues at stake, an enthusiastic desire to formulate positive policies of action and a belief that the work of the Conference members, though successfully inaugurated, was nevertheless only at its beginning. The fruits of Group work and of succeeding Conferences are expected to amplify and develop the initial theses. Moreover, whilst the original balance of opinions and peoples will be preserved, the Conference membership will be steadily increased, and it may be that in due time the members of this new movement (for so it is) will be able to influence substantially the public opinion, and perhaps the official policies, of their respective units of the Commonwealth.

INDEX

MADE AND PRINTED IN GREAT BRITAIN
AT THE BOWERING PRESS, PLYMOUTH